Sexual Harassment,
Work, and Education

SUNY Series, The Psychology of Women
Michele A. Paludi, Editor

Sexual Harassment, Work, and Education

A Resource Manual for Prevention

SECOND EDITION

Michele A. Paludi
and
Richard B. Barickman

State University of New York Press

Published by
State University of New York Press, Albany

© 1998 State University of New York

For information, address State University of New York
Press, State University Plaza, Albany, N.Y., 12246

Production by Diane Ganeles
Marketing by Fran Keneston

Library of Congress Cataloging-in-Publication Data

Paludi, Michele Antoinette.
    Sexual harassment, work, and education : a resource manual for
prevention / Michele A. Paludi and Richard B. Barickman. — 2nd ed.
        p.   cm. — (SUNY series, the psychology of women)
    Rev. ed. of: Academic and workplace sexual harassment. c1991.
    Includes bibliographical references and index.
    ISBN 0-7914-3891-0 (alk. paper). — ISBN 0-7914-3892-9 (pbk. :
alk. paper)
    1. Sexual harassment in universities and colleges—United States.
2. Sex discrimination in employment—United States. 3. Sexual
harassment of women—United States. I. Barickman, Richard.
II. Paludi, Michele Antoinette. Academic and workplace sexual
harassment. III. Title. IV. Series: SUNY series in the psychology
of women.
LC212.862.P35 1998
331.4'133—dc21   97-49416
                                                                              CIP

10 9 8 7 6 5 4 3 2 1

In memory of Reverand Richard Campbell,
whose guidance, wisdom, and support of this book
will always be appreciated.

Michele A. Paludi

For all those who have refused to remain silent
about sexual harassment.

Richard B. Barickman

Contents

Preface

In 1991, we published the first edition of this manual, the first comprehensive resource manual for understanding and preventing sexual harassment in workplaces as well as on college/university campuses. We integrated psychological and legal perspectives in understanding and dealing with sexual harassment, citing numerous empirical research studies as well as practical, effective experiences of human resource managers and affirmative action officers.

We also relied heavily on our own experiences as co-coordinators of the Hunter College Sexual Harassment Panel. Our work on this panel included conducting in-house research on the prevalence of sexual harassment, educating the campus community about the interface of power and gender in the classroom and office setting, and investigating formal and informal complaints of sexual harassment filed by students, faculty, administrators, and staff. Our experience also included conducting training programs for faculty and administrators at several campuses, including William Paterson College, Siena College, Gettysburg College, New York University, and the American Association of Affirmative Action Officers.

From our experiences at Hunter College and other campuses, we recognized the need for a resource manual that not only offered practical suggestions, based on empir-

ical research and experience, on how to offer training programs on sexual harassment; how to develop or revise a
policy statement prohibiting sexual harassment; but also
how to investigate complaints of sexual harassment in a
sensitive way, taking into account the psychology of the
victimization process. From the letters we have received
from human resource specialists and college administrators, who have used our book as well as the number of faculty who used our resource manual in their courses in business and in psychology, we further recognized the
importance of providing updated resources. This second
edition is a direct outgrowth of the responses we have
received from individuals who used our first book.

Another reason we decided to write a second edition of
this resource manual concerns the number of colleges/uni-
versities who implemented at their own campus the program we established at Hunter College for investigating
complaints of sexual harassment. Our work received
national attention through an article written by Debra
Blum for the *Chronicle of Higher Education*. Our program
of education, procedures, and research was also acknowledged by the New York State Branch of the American Association of University Women: we received their Progress in
Equity Award.

We share the new stage of our thinking and application of these perspectives in this second edition of this
resource manual. We also have included some newer
issues, including "consensual relationships" on college
campuses, resources for dealing with sexual harassment in
elementary and secondary schools, and individualized
training programs for individuals who have been found to
have engaged in sexual harassment by their company or
school.

Since the publication of the first edition, Michele
Paludi has left academia full time and is now president of
her own consulting firm that deals specifically with sexual
harassment training, expert witness testimony, research,
and the development of policies and investigatory procedures. To this second edition, Michele brings this experi-

ence as well as her work with former New York State Governor Mario Cuomo and his Task Force on Sexual Harassment. Michele is also the chair of the Subpanel on Sexual Harassment, Violence, and Alcohol and other Drug Abuse in Higher Education, part of the United States Department of Education's gender equity expert panels.

Richard Barickman has implemented many of the suggestions from the first edition of this book in his teaching at the college level and his administrative work (Richard now chairs the department of English at Hunter College).

Many individuals deserve recognition for their participation in our work and lives. We would like to express our appreciation to them for their support, guidance, and assistance: Rosalie Paludi, Lucille Paludi, Fr. John Provost, Luis Beltre, Dennis Stapf Jr., Joan Estes Barickman, Evelyn Barickman, Christopher Barickman, Julia Barickman, Nondita Mason, and Trudith Smoke.

We invite you to contact us with your comments about this second edition as well as with your questions about sexual harassment. Michele Paludi may be reached at 1606 Lenox Road, Schenectady, NY 12308. Richard Barickman may be reached at the Department of English, Hunter College, 695 Park Avenue, New York, NY 10021.

Michele A. Paludi
Richard B. Barickman

CHAPTER 1

What to Do if You Believe
You Have Been Sexually Harassed:
Resources for Individuals

INTRODUCTION

We have written this resource manual primarily for human resource personnel and school/college administrators who want to deal effectively with sexual harassment through the development of policy statements, investigatory procedures, and training/education programs.

Yet we recognize that individuals may also want to know about sexual harassment because of their own experiences with this form of sexual victimization and/or with being involved in a sexual harassment complaint proceeding. We therefore have written this chapter with the goal of assisting individuals who believe they are being sexually harassed. We offer suggestions for resolving complaints within the school/workplace as well as for obtaining therapeutic support in dealing with sexual harassment.

We hope the resources in this chapter will assist individuals in coping with their own sexual harassment experiences. The materials, in this chapter, can also be useful for friends and family members of sexually harassed individuals as well as for individuals who have been accused of sexual harassment.

We present the following material in a question and

answer format. The questions represent the ones we are asked frequently by individuals who believe they are experiencing sexual harassment.

WHAT IS SEXUAL HARASSMENT?

The Equal Employment Opportunity Commission (EEOC) guidelines (see below) state that sexual harassment is "unwelcome sexual advances, requests for sexual favors, and other verbal or physical conduct of a sexual nature" when *any one* of the following criteria is met:

- Submission to such conduct is made either explicitly or implicitly a term or condition of the individual's employment;
- Submission to or rejection of such conduct by an individual is used as the basis for employment decisions affecting the individual;
- Such conduct has the purpose or effect of unreasonably interfering with an individual's work or creating an intimidating, hostile or offensive work environment.

This definition may be extended to academic institutions as well.

There are two types of sexual harassment situations which are described by this EEOC definition: quid pro quo and hostile or discriminatory work environment. The United States Supreme Court has agreed with the agency that both of these situations are violations of the federal law. We will discuss each of these sexual harassment situations separately because they involve different conduct and have their own legal parameters.

Quid pro quo is a legal term which roughly translates to "something for something." Under the EEOC definition, quid pro quo cases involve behavior in which "submission to such conduct is made either explicitly or implicitly a term or condition of an individual's employment [or] submission to or rejection of such conduct by an individual is used as the basis for employment decisions affecting such individual."

Quid pro quo sexual harassment involves an individual with organizational power who expressly or implicitly ties a "term, condition or privilege of employment/education" to the response of an employee/student to unwelcome sexual advances. Thus, failure to receive a promotion, failure to be assigned preferred working hours, threats of being fired, failure to get the grade earned, or retaliatory behavior, such as unjustifiably negative employment evaluations or recommendations all illustrate quid pro quo sexual harassment.

Hostile environment sexual harassment involves a situation where an atmosphere or climate is created in the workplace or school/college that makes it difficult, if not impossible, for an employee/student to work because the atmosphere is perceived by the individual as intimidating, offensive, and hostile.

For sexual harassment to be actionable it must be sufficiently severe or pervasive to alter the conditions of the employee's employment and create an abusive or hostile working environment. The Supreme Court in 1993 ruled that Title VII (see below) may be violated regardless of whether the individual suffered psychological harm in a hostile working environment (*Harris v. Forklift Systems, Inc.*).

In behavioral terms, sexual harassment consists of the sexualization of an instrumental relationship (e.g., supervisor-employee; professor-student) through the introduction of sexist or sexual remarks, requests, or requirements in the context of a formal power differential. Sexual harassment does not fall within the range of personal private relationships. It happens when a person with power in the school or workplace (e.g., professor, dean, supervisor) abuses that power to intimidate, coerce, or humiliate someone because of their sex. It is a breach of trust that is supposed to exist among members of a school or workplace. Sexual harassment is unwelcome and introduces a sexual element into what should be a professional situation.

Verbal harassment includes:

a. unwelcome sexual innuendos, comments, and sexual remarks
b. suggestive, obscene, or insulting sounds
c. implied or overt threats
d. pressure for sex

Physical harassment includes:

a. unwelcome patting, pinching, and brushing up against the body
b. coerced sexual intercourse
c. assault
d. leering or ogling
e. obscene gestures

ISN'T SEXUAL HARASSMENT THE SAME AS FLIRTING?

No! If someone is flirting with you, flattering you, or paying you compliments, you can exercise freedom of choice in deciding whether to establish a close, intimate relationship. This freedom of choice is absent in sexual harassment. In addition, flirting makes the receiver feel good, in control, and attractive. Sexual harassment makes the receiver feel uncomfortable, anxious, threatened. Let's deal with the impact of sexual harassment in more detail.

HOW CAN I EXPECT TO FEEL IF I AM BEING SEXUALLY HARASSED?

Not everyone will respond the same way to being sexually harassed, but research has suggested the following responses that are most commonly experienced by victims of sexual harassment (also see chapters 2, 3, and 4):

Career Effects

    a. Changes in study/work habits
    b. Drop in school/work performance because of stress
    c. Absenteeism
    d. Withdrawal from school/work
    e. Changes in career goals

Emotional Reactions

    a. Shock, denial
    b. Anger, frustration
    c. Insecurity, embarrassment
    d. Confusion, self-consciousness
    e. Shame, powerlessness
    f. Guilt, isolation

Physical Reactions

    a. Headaches
    b. Inability to concentrate
    c. Sleep disturbances
    d. Lethargy
    e. Gastrointestinal distress
    f. Respiratory problems
    g. Phobias, panic reactions
    h. Nightmares
    i. Eating disorders
    j. Dermatological reactions

Changes in Self-Perception

    a. Poor self-concept/self-esteem
    b. Lack of competency
    c. Powerlessness
    d. Isolation

Social, Interpersonal Relatedness, and Sexual Effects

    a. Withdrawal
    b. Fear of new people

   c. Lack of trust
   d. Change in physical appearance
   e. Change in social network patterns
   f. Negative attitudes about sexual relationships

These responses are influenced by disappointment in the way others react to your experiences; the stress of harassment-induced life changes such as moves, loss of income, and disrupted work history. Legal expenses, medical costs, and psychotherapy costs contribute to these responses as well.

We recommend seeking medical attention and psychotherapeutic support (see below). Tell your physician and mental health practitioner about your experiences and perceptions about these experiences.

IS IT COMMON FOR PEOPLE TO CONFRONT THE INDIVIDUAL THEY BELIEVE IS SEXUALLY HARASSING THEM?

Some people feel comfortable in confronting the alleged harasser. Others remain silent for fear of possible retaliation should they speak out about their experiences. This latter response is very common among individuals who work at an organization or attend a school/college that does not have an effective and enforced policy statement prohibiting sexual harassment.

As we discuss throughout this resource manual, researchers classify individuals' responses into two categories: internally focused strategies and externally focused strategies. Internal strategies represent attempts to manage the emotions and thoughts associated with the behaviors individuals have experienced. The following are examples of internally focused strategies.

Detachment. You minimize the situation, treat it as a joke.

Denial. You deny behaviors; attempt to forget about it.

Relabeling. You reappraise situation as less threatening; offer excuses for harasser's behaviors.

Illusory Control. You attempt to take responsibility for harassment.

Endurance. You put up with behavior because you do not believe help is available or you fear retaliation.

Externally focused strategies focus on the harassing situation itself, including reporting the behavior to the individual charged with investigating complaints of sexual harassment. The following are examples of externally focused strategies:

Avoidance. You attempt to avoid the situation by staying away from the harasser.

Assertion / Confrontation. You refuse sexual or social offers or verbally confront the harasser.

Seeking Institutional / Organizational Relief. You report the incident and file a complaint.

Social Support. You seek support of others to validate perceptions of the behaviors.

Appeasement. You attempt to evade the harasser without confrontation; attempt to placate the harasser

You may find yourself identifying with one strategy at the outset of your experiences and, with time, decide another strategy would work better. We recommend discussing your options with a trusted family member and/or friend as well as the organization's or school's representative for handling complaints of sexual harassment. Your school or workplace should have an individual, e.g., sexual harassment advisor or employee assistance program counselor, who can answer questions for you about the complaint procedure prior to you actually filing a complaint.

Research has also suggested that you may feel the following when you are experiencing sexual harassment:

- Confused and/or embarassed
- Helpless
- Angry and/or insulted
- Worried

Share these concerns with your sexual harassment advisor. You may view yourself as needy, frightened, weak, and out of control. Perhaps you didn't see yourself as a potential victim. Have you asked "Why me?" "I didn't do anything to lead this person on." "I wasn't dressed provocatiely." These are common responses from an individual who has experienced sexual harassment.

Women and men who have been sexually harassed typically experience physical and emotional damage. They also suffer negative impact on their career advancement. Many lose jobs or promotions, get low grades in school, change academic programs, or mistrust educational opportunities which they previously found appealing and promising.

Because sexual harassment is still not publicly acknowledged as a major form of abuse, people often respond to sexual harassment with confusion, doubt, self-blame, and a desire to flee the situation rather than report it.

HOW CAN I CONFRONT THE INDIVIDUAL I BELIEVE IS SEXUALLY HARASSING ME?

We will summarize three main strategies for dealing with sexual harassment: individual, institutional, and legal.

Individual Strategy

Affirmative Action Officer, Mary Rowe, at the Massachusetts Institute of Technology, suggests that writing a letter to the perceived harasser frequently stops the harassment. She recommends that the letter consist of three sections:

1. A factual account that indicates what happened.
2. A description of the way the writer feels about the events that occurred.

3. A statement of what the writer wants to happen next.

In table 1.1 we present a sample letter. Rowe also recommends that the letter be delivered in person or by registered or certified mail.

Table 1.1
Writing a Letter to a Perceived Harasser

Factual Account of What Happened

We recommend the letter begin with a factual, non-evaluative description of the events that took place. This section should be as detailed as possible, including dates, places, people present, and a description of the incidents. For example, "On Wednesday, May 24, during your office hours (2–4 P.M.), I came to discuss the grade you put on my term paper (B–). During the course of our discussion you patted my thigh and hugged me twice."

Description of Feelings about Incident

In this section, you need to document your feelings about the events described in the first section. For example, "My stomach turned to knots during my visit with you in your office hours"; "I am afraid to come to a department meeting because I don't want you to ever touch me or look at me the way you did."

What Writer Wants to Happen Next

In this section you need to express what you would like to happen next. For example, "I don't ever want you to touch me or hug me again."

After this letter is completed and sent, it is advisable to:

- Not send copies of this letter to the press or college/workplace administrators.
- Keep at least one copy of the letter.
- Not discuss the letter with the person if you do not want to.

You may also use these recommendations in confronting the individual in person. You may want to rehearse your comments with a friend and/or the sexual harassment advisor. We offer the following suggestions:

Communicate the following:

What you are feeling, for example:

- The behavior that you find offensive.
- That you expect the offensive behavior to stop.
- That you want an apology.
- That you are prepared to file a complaint within the company/school should the offensive behavior continue.

Take along a friend for support. This person should remain quiet during the meeting.

Keep a record of the following:

- What was said by each individual.
- How you felt after the confrontation.
- Whether the individual apologized to you.
- Your friend's perceptions of the exchange.
- How the individual responded to you.

Share this record with the friend who supported you and/or a trusted friend. Keep this record for documentation purposes should you need to file an internal complaint.

Writing a letter to or meeting with the perceived harasser can be a successful individual strategy for the following reasons:

- It helps you gain a sense of control over the situation.
- It breaks a pattern of silence you may have kept out of fear of retaliation and/or disbelief.
- It maintains confidentiality.
- It provides an individual with information about the way their behavior is being interpreted by you.

- It most likely avoids formal charges and a public confrontation.
- It suggests that you are willing to take action to stop the harassment.

Should you choose these options, we recommend you write this letter or rehearse your comments with the advice of an individual who handles sexual harassment advising at your school or workplace.

Institutional Strategies

The following questions need to be addressed when dealing with sexual harassment in schools or the workplace:

Does the institution have a policy dealing with sexual harassment?

It should be available from your human resource office, dean of students, or affirmative action office. The policy should also be printed in employees/student handbooks. Familiarize yourself with this policy statement. Look for the following components (also see chapters 2, 3, and 4) for additional issues regarding policy statements):

- Statement Prohibiting Sexual Harassment.
- Legal Definitions of Sexual Harassment.
- Behavioral Examples of Sexual Harassment.
- Statement of School/Workplace's Responsibility in Resolving Complaints of Sexual Harassment.
- Statement of Students'/Employees' Responsibility in Filing Complaints.
- Statement of Sanctions.
- Statement Concerning Sanctions for Retaliation.
- Statement Concerning False Complaints.
- Identification of Individual(s) Responsible for Hearing Complaints.

Is there an informal procedure to help resolve complaints prior to formal charges?

Copies of investigatory procedures should be available from administrators at the school/workplace. Familiarize yourself with the following components of the investigatory procedures:

- How Confidentiality will be Maintained.
- Role and Responsibility of Witnesses for Either Complainant or Accused.
- Statute of Limitations in Filing Complaint.
- Who will Conduct the Investigation of Your Complaint.
- Educational Qualifications of Investigators.
- Amount of Time to Complete Investigation of Complaint.
- How Closure will be Provided to All Parties.
- Names of Individuals at Your Institution who Can Assist You in Preparing Your Complaint.

We also recommend the following for individuals who believe they are experiencing sexual harassment:

- Keep a diary of all experiences with the person you believe is harassing you, including any witnesses present, precise dates and times, copies of notes, and so forth.
- Recognize that using an institutional strategy can be intimidating—these procedures take time and often involve considerable embarassment and stress for all parties.
- Inquire as to whether you need outside resources to help you resolve the complaint. If so, ask how you obtain them.

WHAT IF IF AM UNHAPPY WITH THE OUTCOME OF THE INVESTIGATION AT MY WORKPLACE?

We recommend that you try to resolve complaints of sexual harassment within the workplace according to the policy statement. But if you are dissatisified with the outcome of the internal investigation or have reason to believe you are not receiving fair treatment during the internal investigation, other recourse is available. We discuss one in detail in the following section: The Equal Employment Opportunity Commission. This mode of resolution is for workplace sexual harassment. We will later discuss additional means of resolutions for academic sexual harassment.

Legal Strategies

What is Title VII? Title VII of the Civil Rights Act of 1964 prohibits employment discrimination on the basis of sex, race, color, religion, and national origin.

Who is Covered by Title VII? Title VII covers all employers who employ fifteen or more employees. Title VII also covers employees who work in educational institutions.

Who Enforces Title VII? The Equal Employment Opportunity Commission (EEOC) was created by the Civil Rights Act of 1964. It was granted the authority to investigate and conciliate complaints that alleged a violation of the law of employment discrimination.

Has the EEOC Issued any Guidelines for Employers? Yes, In 1980, the EEOC issued interpretive guidelines on sexual harassment under Title VII. These guidelines stated that:

- Title VII prohibits sexual harassment of employees.
- Employers are responsible for the actions of their agents and supervisors.
- Employers are responsible for the actions of all other employees if the employer knew or should have known about the sexual harassment.

What Must Employers Do to Comply with the Guidelines?

The guidelines state that an employer should take all necessary steps to prevent sexual harassment such as:

- *Affirmatively discussing sexual harassment.*
- *Expressing strong disapproval of sexual harassment.*
- *Developing sanctions for individuals who have engaged in sexual harassment.*
- *Informing employees of their right to raise and how to raise the issue of sexual harassment.*
- *Training employees concerning what constitutes sexual harassment.*

Under the Guidelines, are Employers Liable for Sexual Harassment?

Yes. These guidelines hold employers fully responsible for the actions of their employees.

How Can the EEOC Help Me if I am Dissatisfied with My Company's Investigation?

In order to use the protections and benefits of Title VII of the U.S. Civil Rights Act, you must file a claim with the Equal Employment Opportunity Commission (EEOC). Because this statute applies only to companies with fifteen employees or more, you must be sure that your company qualifies. The law states that the required number of employees must be employed "in each of 20 or more calendar weeks in the current or preceding calendar year." So a business with ten people currently employed might still qualify, if five or more additional people worked the required twenty weeks in the current or preceding year. Title VII measures in weeks not days or months, so if fifteen employees work regularly during a week, even though not every day, the business qualifies under Title VII. Employees who work twenty or more hours a week are definitely counted. If the business regularly employs a number of part-time people, then they *may* be counted (courts have varied in their willingness to count part-time employees). Once it is determined by the EEOC or a court that a company is large enough to be included in the law's provisions, then all employees are covered, no matter how many hours per week or weeks per year they work.

Sometimes an employee is designated an "independent contractor" by an employer and asked to sign a document to that effect. Courts have held that you must control not just the product of your work but also the process—where and when you work, for example—to be a truly independent contractor. Generally, you are considered an employee under Title VII if you do not have true independent control over this process. For example, if you are hired to make telephone solicitations as an "independent contractor" but are required to make these calls during a specified time at a specified place, you are not a true independent contractor and are thus an employee under Title VII's terms.

How Do I File a Complaint with the EEOC?

You may file a sexual harassment or sexual discrimination claim at any EEOC office, by yourself or with the assistance of an attorney or other advisor. The claim must be written. You may also file your claim by mail. We advise using certified mail as a guarantee of delivery, especially if you are nearing a filing deadline. There is no charge for filing. Though it is ordinarily advisable to file a claim at the EEOC office nearest you, legally you may file at any office.

We advise filing in person, unless some compelling circumstance—such as the need to maintain anonymity—prevents you. Personal filing insures that your claim has been received. You also establish a personal connection with some of the agency's staff and can inquire about investigative procedures, filing deadlines, and so forth. And when you file in person, you can use the charge form the EEOC has designed, which may expedite the investigation.

The EEOC allows another person or organization (such as a union, an Employee Assistance Program, a women's advocacy group) to file the claim on your behalf in order to protect your anonymity. This procedure is designed not only to maintain confidentiality and protect you from retaliation while the investigation proceeds, but also to encourage employees to file complaints promptly.

What is the Time Limit for My Filing
My Complaint with the EEOC?

The EEOC has two different time limits (statute of limitations) for filing claims, 180 days and 300 days, dating from the sexual harassment incident(s) in your claim. It's best to assume you have only 180 days to file, unless you are explicitly told otherwise by the EEOC. In any case, you should usually file as soon as possible so that the investigation can begin while witnesses' memories are fresh and so that any continued or threatened sexual harassment can be curtailed.

NOTE: The EEOC does not extend the time limit for accepting your claim because you first attempted to resolve your conflict through a company complaint procedure. You may, however, file a claim with the EEOC and ask them to defer any investigation until after you have completed a company procedure for resolving complaints of sexual harassment.

How Do I Write My Claim?

You do not have to submit your claim on a special form (though using the EEOCs forms may provide you with more of the information you need, in a more accesible format). According to EEOC regulations, the claim should include:

1. The full name, address, and telephone number of the person making the complaint, or of the person or organization filing a confidential complaint;
2. The full name or names and addresses of those charged with harassment, if known;
3. A clear, concise statement of the facts that constitute sexual harassment, including dates when the harassment occurred;
4. The approximate number of employees in the business where you work, if you know.

In naming those charged in your claim, you should ordinarily include both the name of the person or people who harassed you and the name of your employer (including the names of any parent company, franchiser, or affiliate). When you write your claim:

1. Give all the important facts, including relevant behavior and attitudes that may support your claim;
2. State the facts to your position, without doubts or qualifications that could weaken your claim ("Maybe I should have said something the first time he touched me.");
3. Be conscious of the 180–day filing limit and make sure that at least some of the acts of harassment you cite fall within this period;
4. Be concise. You should cover all important facts and circumstances, but the EEOC will interview you to obtain a fuller account when they investigate the claim.

Can I Inquire About the Status of My Claim?

Yes. EEOC offices vary considerably in caseloads, procedures, and quality of personnel. Only a small percentage of the complaints the EEOC receive ever reach the courts—as few as 1 percent. Inquire regularly about the status of the EEOC investigation of your case. If you have an attorney, the attorney should also follow the investigation closely and periodically contact the agency. If you are concerned about the handling of your case, speak with appropriate personnel at the EEOC office. If you are unhappy with the quality of the investigation, request that your case be assigned to a new investigator.

Will My Complaint Be Anonymous?

You may not be able to maintain anonymity, even though the EEOC keeps your identity confidential. Because your claim must give very precise details and name particular individuals and incidents, it will often be easy for employers, managers, and supervisors to determine your identity—and they are not legally bound to maintain confidentiality. Retaliation becomes a very real possibility. Report any indications of retaliation to the EEOC immediately and ask them to take protective action if necessary. Often the EEOC may suggest conciliation or some other agreement with the employer to resolve the complaint, and this usually requires disclosing your identity. If a solution seems near, this may not be problematic, but if it is a problem, try to get a commitment from the EEOC that it will go to court, if necessary, to prevent the employer from retaliating against you.

Can Investigations be Made by the EEOC Without Complaints?

The EEOC will only conduct investigations if charges have been filed.

How Do I Determine the Date when the Harassment Began?

The standard 180-day limit on filing your claim begins on the day the sexual harassment occurs, according to EEOC regulations. But determining this date can be problematic and crucial, since the ability to take advantage of Title VIIs provisions depends upon it. Consider the following hypothetical circumstances:

A few weeks after you are promoted to a new position within your company, you begin to find pornographic photos and ads on your desk. You say nothing, hoping that whoever is putting them there will stop if you show no reaction. You are very upset, however, especially since you are new to this office and have no one there you can trust as yet. After a few more weeks this harassment stops. About a month later a co-worker with whom you have become friendly tells you that she saw another coworker putting one of the photos on your desk. She tells you that he is notorious for making sexual advances toward new female employees, and you confide in her that he has in fact made obnoxious sexual advances to you on several occasions. You avoid this man as much as you can and try not to be alone with him. Unfortunately, you are assigned to work on a project with him about five months later (the prospect makes you extremely uncomfortable and apprehensive). After a few weeks, while you are working together early in the morning, trying to meet a deadline, he grabs you and begins kissing and fondling you. You manage to get free and leave the office. Later, after your supervisor has arrived, you report the whole set of circumstances to him. He laughs and says that Gerry is a little obnoxious but harmless. "You'll get used to him," he declares. When you persist in demanding action to stop the harassment, your supervisor tells you that if you're unhappy, you can always ask for a transfer to your previous position (a demotion). After several weeks of anxiety, conversations with friends, and unsuccessful efforts to get assistance from the company's personnel office, you decide to file a complaint with the EEOC.

More than six months have passed since the first act of harassment (the first obscene photo on your desk). So if you date the harassment from this act, the 180-day time limit has expired. If you consider the act of harassment the sexual assault, you are well within the limit. You can use receiving the first obscene photo as evidence of a long pattern of harassing behavior, worsening the impact of the sexual assault you cite as the occasion of your claim.

There are several circumstances that may persuade the EEOC or the courts to allow you to file a claim beyond the deadline. The EEOC may extend the filing deadline if you have a compelling reason—such as illness—that made it impossible for you to file on time. If you can demonstrate that you were misinformed about the motives behind certain key events relevant to your claim, you may be able to obtain an exension, if you file promptly once you discover the truth. For example, you may be laid off or transferred after you resist or report sexual harassment, ostensibly because of company labor needs but actually, you later learn, in retaliation for your response to the harassment. If your employer misleads you about your rights under the law in a way that causes you to delay filing a claim, you may also be granted an extension to file.

How Would the EEOC Investigate My Complaint?

The EEOC will contact the employer and the people specifically charged with sexual harassment within ten days after the claim is filed, usually by sending them a copy of your claim. They then have the right to file their own versions of the events decribed in the claim. Witnesses for either side may also submit written testimony.

NOTE: A victim has a right to see all information the EEOC obtains through its investigation and may use that information as evidence in any court proceedings.

The EEOC may request more information from you, through interviews or through a more detailed written statement. You may be asked to sit down with your employer and EEOC investigators in a fact-finding conference, to see what facts are agreed on.

The EEOC can seek a court order to protect you from retaliation by your employer while the investigation is ongoing. Although such legal action is not common, if you experience retaliation or threats of retaliation, you should report it to the agency and ask them to take protective action, including a court order, if necessary.

The EEOC also has subpoena power, often crucial in obtaining documents in employer files relating to your job performance, investigative reports of sexual harassment, personnel files to compare with your own performance reports, and so forth. A subpoena may also be used to force your employer or other witnesses to testify.

Once the investigation is complete, the EEOC decides either to attempt an informal settlement of the claim (conciliation) or to dismiss the case. If the agency finds that there are reasonable grounds to believe you have been sexually harassed, it will attempt conciliation. Ordinarily, the first step in this process is for you to determine what restitution and/or compensation you want. Once the EEOC knows what resolution you would like, it attempts to persuade the employer to give you whatever a court would grant if you won the case. The agency has no authority in this process of conciliation to force you to accept anything less than your full legal rights. You may, of course, voluntarily agree to accept less. If you and your employer agree to the negotiated settlement (usually including a requirement that the employer end its illegal practices), the case is resolved. The EEOC will continue to monitor the case to insure that the employer complies with the terms of the settlement.

If the employer rejects the settlement, then the EEOC will issue a right-to-sue letter that allows you to file your own lawsuit. The records of the conciliation remain confidential (unlike the records of the EEOC's investigation), and may not be used or referred to in any court action.

If the EEOC finds that you have not provided sufficient evidence to support your claim of sexual harassment, the office issues a "no cause determination." You have the right not only to appeal such a decision but also initiate a lawsuit just as if you had received a "right-to-sue letter," however, the employer may use the EEOC's "no cause" judgment as evidence that you were not harassed.

How Long Does an Investigation by the EEOC Take?

The EEOC is supposed to complete its investigation within 180 days after a claim is filed. The investigation may take longer. Unless you demand a "right-to-sue" letter during this lengthy investigation, the EEOC will not issue one, preferring to wait until the investigation and efforts at conciliation have been completed. Since you cannot sue without this letter (or without a finding of "no cause") and since you cannot know how long the investigation will take, you may want to demand a "right-to-sue" letter before the investigation is over if you have decided to pursue your claim in court.

You have ninety days from the date you receive the right-to-sue letter to file a lawsuit; so it is important that you reach your decision about a lawsuit carefully and file the suit promptly if that is your decision. The EEOC ordinarily stops its investigation when it issues a right-to-sue letter, so you should make sure that the investigation has disclosed enough evidence that supports the claim to make a convincing case in court. You should also have consulted and retained an attorney experienced in sexual harassment law who is prepared to file a lawsuit quickly.

Is Retaliation for Filing an EEOC Complaint Illegal?

Employers are prohibited from retaliating against an employee who filed a complaint with the EEOC or assisted with an investigation of another employee's complaint.

Does the EEOC Prohibit Sexual Harassment of Students?

The EEOC guidelines apply to employees. Students who are also employees are covered by the guidelines, however.

What Guidelines are Offered for Students?

The Federal statute that applies to sexual harassment in education is Title IX of the 1972 Educational Amendments. Title IX was passed to prohibit sex discrimination in higher education. Title IX is enforced by the Office of Civil Rights (OCR) of the United States Department of Education. Title IX states:

> no person in the United States shall, on the basis of sex, be excluded from participation in, be denied the benefits of, or be subjected to discrimination under any educational program or activity receiving Federal financial assistance.

Thus, the sanction threatened against an educational institution found in violation of Title IX is the withdrawal of federal funds. Also under the regulations of Title IX, educational institutions must establish procedures through which students who are victims of sex discrimination can complain.

WHAT IF THERE IS NO POLICY STATEMENT AGAINST SEXUAL HARASSMENT AT MY SCHOOL/WORKPLACE?

In the event that you do not have a policy statement and thus investigatory procedures for dealing with sexual harassment, contact the following for information and suggestions:

- Your Local Office of the Equal Employment Opportunity Commission
- Your State Division of Human Rights
- Your State Board of Education

WHAT KINDS OF THERAPEUTIC SUPPORT IS AVAILABLE— IF I FILE OR DON'T FILE A COMPLAINT IN MY SCHOOL/WORKPLACE?

Seeking resolution for a complaint of sexual harassment can be upsetting and anger-provoking for individuals. Very often individuals want some therapeutic support to help them deal with the victimization in general and the resolution of the complaint specifically.

What kinds of counselors are available?
- Psychologists
- Psychiatrists
- Psychiatric Social Workers
- Psychiatric Nurses
- Pastoral Counselors

What are the backgrounds of these counselors?

- Psychologists have received graduate training in diagnosing and treating a range of emotional problems and mental disorders. They are specialists in either clinical psychology, counseling psychology, or school psychology.
- Psychiatrists are physicians with a specialization in emotional disorders. They are the only counselors who are permitted to prescribe medication (e.g., antidepressants).
- Psychiatric social workers have earned a master's degree or doctorate in a program that emphasizes mental health and counseling.
- Psychiatric nurses have received training in a school of nursing and have medical training.
- Pastoral counselors include priests, ministers, rabbis, nuns, and other religious individuals who have received training in counseling or therapeutic intervention.

HOW CAN I TELL IF A COUNSELOR IS QUALIFIED TO HELP ME?

Prior to working with any professional counselor, you should know the following about the individual: his/her training, experience, and licensing status. If the professional is licensed, you should contact the state licensing board to confirm this information. If the professional is not licensed, you may seek additional information about this individual from local organizations/agencies, for example, the Rape Crisis Center, Battered Women's Shelter, YWCA, or College/University Counseling Center.

DO COUNSELORS SPECIALIZE IN SEXUAL HARASSMENT?

Many counselors specialize in sexual harassment. You can inquire about a counselor's specialization by asking the counselor personally or through referrals from the agencies listed above.

WHAT SHOULD I EXPECT FROM A COUNSELOR?

A counselor should:

1. assess the severity of your immediate crisis.
2. validate the seriousness of your experience.
3. evaluate your degree of depressive, psychosomatic, anxiety, and post-traumatic stress symptoms.
4. allow you to explore and express your feelings.
5. support your existing coping strategies.
6. facilitate new coping skills.
7. facilitate a plan of action for you to regain a sense of control.
8. assess any prior victimization experiences that compound the present one.
9. support you during every step of the litigation process.

If you are worried about any testimony you are to give in the resolution of your complaint, ask your counselor to work with you in visualizing yourself successfully surviving testimony and helping you to remain calm when asked uncomfortable questions.

**ARE THERE SUPPORT GROUPS FOR
VICTIMS OF SEXUAL HARASSMENT?**

The goals of a support group for victims of sexual harassment should include the following:

Goals:

• Listen to and respect individuals' reactions to being sexually harassed.

- Sort out sound choices with respect to dealing with sexual harassment.
- Be aware of the commonality of themes in group members' lives.
- Define quid pro quo and hostile environment sexual harassment.
- Discuss psychological issues involved in dealing with sexual harassment.
- Discuss the physical and emotional reactions to sexual harassment.
- Provide a psychological profile of sexual harassers.
- Discuss peer sexual harassment.
- Discuss means of resolution for complaints of sexual harassment.
- Assess perceptions of the definition, incidence, and psychological dimensions of sexual harassment.

In support groups on sexual harassment, each participant should be given a list of responsibilities—what is expected of them in the support group. For example:

- Support group members agree to avoid judging one another and focus on support and positive statements to each person, even when making a difficult comment.
- Time arrangements (both beginning and end) are agreed upon and honored by all members.
- Any confronting is clear, gentle, and nurturing.
- Members agree to come every time unless it is impossible to do so.
- Confidential information must never be relayed to others outside a support group.
- Individual privacy must be respected at all times.
- An atmosphere of safety and security must be maintained at all times.
- Each individual has the responsibility of taking care of her/himself.

**WILL KNOWLEDGE OF MY SEEKING THERAPEUTIC SUPPORT
BE USED IN THE RESOLUTION OF COMPLAINTS?**

In all probability, yes. This circumstance is often used
to support the plaintiff's claim of psychological trauma. It
may seem like a *Catch 22* situation: You want and need the
support in dealing with sexual harassment and its related
issues. You don't want this fact to be used against you
either at your school/company or in the courts. There isn't
an easy answer here. It must be an individual decision. We
can point out, however, that individuals, who have sought
therapy, feel better about themselves and have welcomed
the opportunity to deal with the victimization and complaint procedure with a supportive counselor.

**HOW CAN I FIND OUT ABOUT ORGANIZATIONS
THAT FOCUS ATTENTION ON SEXUAL HARASSMENT?**

You can write to any of the organizations listed in
table 1.2 for additional information regarding sexual
harassment in academic or workplace settings. For information regarding 1-800 numbers, contact the Toll Free
Directory published by AT&T. We also recommend consulting the following directory of organizations in the United
States: *Encyclopedia of Associations*. It is published by
Gale Research Inc., 835 Penobscot Bldg. Detrot, MI 48226.

A recommended new directory of women's organizations, entitled *The Women's Information Exchange National
Directory* was compiled by Deborah Brecher and Jill Lippitt
and published by Avon Books.

**WHAT CAN I DO TO HELP IMPROVE LEGISLATION
AGAINST SEXUAL HARASSMENT?**

We recommend speaking with and writing to local,
state, and federal legislators about the improvement of

sexual harassment legislation. We offer some suggestions for this purpose.

Contacting Legislators

A personal visit or a personal letter are the most effective ways of letting elected representatives know that their voting record on sexual harassment is being monitored. Written communication and visits are counted, catalogued, and answered by legislative aids who *tally* their district's opinion.

Information about contacting your legislators is presented in table 1.3.

WHAT KINDS OF SOCIAL AND VOLUNTEER CLUBS COULD I JOIN FOR SUPPORT?

We recommend participating in local organizations that have sexual harassment as one of their platform or legislative agendas. Supportive individuals participate in these organizations. Check with directory assistance for the local branch of the following organizations:

- American Association of University Women
- Soroptimists International
- Zonta
- League of Women Voters
- Business and Professional Women
- YMCA and YWCA
- Boy Scouts and Girl Scouts
- Rape Crisis Center
- Displaced Homemaker Center
- American Civil Liberties Union
- National Organization for Women

We recommend reading the subsequent chapters in this resource manual for additional information related to sexual harassment in the workplace, college, elementary, and secondary schools.

Table 1.2
Organizations Concerned with Sexual Harassment

9 to 5
 YWCA
 140 Clarendon St.
 Boston, MA 02139

Equal Employment Opportunity Commission
 2401 E Street NW
 Washington, DC 20506

National Organization for Victim Assistance
 1757 Park Rd. NW
 Washington, DC 20010

Equal Rights Advocates
 1663 Mission Street
 Suite 550
 San Francisco, CA 94103

NOW Legal Defense and Education Fund
 99 Hudson Street
 New York, NY 10013

African American Women in Defense of Ourselves
 1111 16th St. NW
 Washington, DC 20036

Women Employed
 22 West Monroe
 Suite 1400
 Chicago, IL 60603

**Liason for Minorities and Women
in Higher Education**
 Office of Women in Higher Education
 One Dupont Circle NW
 Washington, DC 20036

Business and Professional Women's Foundation
 2012 Massachusetts Ave. NW
 Washington, DC 20036

United States Department of Labor
 Women's Bureau
 Washington, DC 20210

**Federation of Organizations
for Professional Women**
2000 P St. NW
Washington, DC 20036

National Council for Research on Women
530 Broadway
New York, NY 10012

Women's Rights Litigation Clinic
Rutgers Law School
15 Washington St.
Newark, NJ 07102

**Table 1.3
Contacting Legislators about Sexual Harassment**

For United States Senators:
The Honorable _____
c/o United States Senate
Washington, DC 20510

For United States Representatives:
The Honorable _____
c/o United States House of Representatives
Washington, DC 20515

For State Senators:
The Honorable _____
c/o Legislative Office Building
City, State, Zip Code

For State Assembly members:
The Honorable _____
c/o Legislative Office Building
City, State, Zip Code

Information about the status of any bill introduced in the United States Senate, or House of Representatives may be obtained by phoning: 202-225-1772.

An individual's opinion about a bill may be registered with the President of the United States by phoning 202-456-1111.

Additional information may be obtained by phoning the League of Women Voters at 1-800-836-6975.

REFERENCES

Duhon, D. 1993. "Sexual Harassment in the Workplace: A Review of the Legal Rights and Responsibilities of All Parties." *Public Personnel Management* 22: 123–135.

Fitzgerald, L. F. 1993. "Sexual Harassment: Violence Against Women in the Workplace. *American Psychologist* 48: 1070–1076.

Levy, A., and M. Paludi. 1997. *Workplace Sexual Harassment.* Englewood Cliffs, NJ: Prentice Hall.

Petrocelli, W., and B. Repa. 1995. *Sexual Harassment on the Job: What It Is and How to Stop It.* Berkeley, CA: Nolo Press.

Sumrall, A., and D. Taylor, eds. 1992. *Sexual Harassment: Women Speak Out.* Freedom, CA: Crossing Press.

CHAPTER 2

Sexual Harassment in Workplaces

INCIDENCE OF SEXUAL HARASSMENT IN THE WORKPLACE

Sexual harassment in the workplace is widespread (Levy and Paludi 1997). Women are more likely to experience sexual harassment than men. For example, the United States Merit Systems Protection Board (1981) addressed sexual harassment in the federal workplace and found that 42 percent of all women employees reported being sexually harassed. Merit Systems reported that many incidents occurred repeatedly, were of long duration, and had a sizeable practical impact, costing the government an estimated minimum of $189 million over the two year period covered by the research project.

Results also indicated that 33 percent of the women reported receiving unwanted sexual remarks, 28 percent reported suggestive looks, and 26 percent reported being deliberately touched. These behaviors were classified in the study as "less severe" types of sexual harassment. When "more severe" forms of sexual harassment were addressed, 15 percent of the women reported experiencing pressure for dates, 9 percent reported being directly pressured for sexual favors, and 9 percent had received unwanted letters and telephone calls. One percent of the sample had experienced actual or attempted rape or assault. Merit Systems repeated their study of workplace sexual harassment in 1987 and reported identical results to their 1981 findings.

Research by Barbara Gutek (1985), with women in the civilian workplace, reports similar findings as well, that is, that approximately half the female workforce experiences sexual harassment. Based on telephone interviews generated through random digit dialing procedures, Gutek's results suggest that 53 percent of working women have reported one incident of sexual harassment during their working lives, including degrading, insulting comments (15 percent), sexual touching (24 percent), socializing expected as part of the job requirement (11 percent), and expected sexual activity (8 percent).

Group differences in sexual harassment were common. Louise F. Fitzgerald and her colleagues (1988), for example, found that women, who were employed in a university setting (e.g., faculty, staff, and administrators) were more likely to experience sexual harassment than were women students in the same institution. Y. Gold (1987) reported that her sample of blue-collar tradeswomen experienced significantly higher levels of all forms of sexual harassment (e.g., gender harassment, seductive behavior, sexual bribery, sexual coercion, sexual assault) than did either white-collar professional women or pink-collar clerical women.

E. LaFontaine and L. Tredeau (1986) reported similar findings in their sample of 160 women, who were all college graduates employed in male-populated occupations (e.g., engineering and management). Nancy Baker (1989) studied a sample of 100 women employed in either traditional or nontraditional occupations, where traditionality was defined by the sex distribution in the work group. Baker also divided the traditional group into pink- and blue-collar workers.The pink-collar group included women who were secretaries and clerical workers. The blue-collar group included women who were industrial workers. Baker reported that high levels of sexual harassment were associated with having low numbers of women in the work group. For example, machinists reported significantly high frequencies of all levels of sexual harassment, whereas the traditional blue-collar workers reported very low levels. Clerical women reported experiences that were more similar to those of the traditional blue-collar workers than the nontraditional blue-collar workers. Baker also reported that women in the pink-collar and traditional blue-collar groups encountered just as many men as the machinists during the workday, but were treated differently. Thus, these results suggested that as women approach numerical parity in various segments of the workforce, sexual harassment declined.

Another perspective also has been raised by Gutek (1985). She has argued that sexual harassment is more likely to occur in occupations in which "sex-role spillover" has occurred. Gutek's model suggests that when occupations are dominated by one sex or the other, the sex role of the dominant sex influences (i.e., spills over) the work role expectations for that job. For example, gender stereotypes imply that men should be sexually aggressive and women ready and willing to be sex objects. Thus, sexual harassment can occur when these gender stereotypes carry over or "spill over" into the workplace setting. Thus, when individuals act on their thoughts about women and men, they may engage in behavior that is discriminatory. For example, research suggests that women are evaluated less favorably than men for identical performance on a job (Doyle and Paludi 1995). In addition, men tend to turn away from women and also to move away from them in contrast to their behavior toward other men (Lott 1990). Furthermore, men have higher expectations for other men's ability than for women's ability; thus, they attribute women's successful performance on the job to luck, cheating, sexuality, or the fact that someone "likes" them. The causal attribution of "lack of ability," however, is used by men to describe women's job performance that is anything but perfect (Gutek and Koss 1993; Levy and Paludi 1997).

The workplace is not insulated from gender stereotyping. For example, women employees not only can be evaluated by their coworkers and supervisors in terms of their sexuality, but also by their performance as sex objects instead of their merit as a manager or colleague. Gender stereotypes are related to the amount of perceived power one has in the workplace. Stereotypes are more commonly used in describing the behavior of those who are seen as having less power in the organization and thus occupy lower-echelon positions.

WHO HARASSES?

Research suggests that men are more likely to engage in sexual harassment than are women. Men who sexually harass are not distinguishable from their colleagues who don't harass with respect to the following variables: age, marital status, occupation, or job status (Fitzgerald and Weitzman, 1990). Men who harass do so repeatedly to many women, especially when they have not received any training and counseling about the impact of their behavior on other individuals. And, men who harass hold attitudes toward women that are traditional, not egalitarian (Zalk 1996).

John Pryor's (1987) research suggested that sexual harassment bears a conceptual similarity to rape. He developed a series of hypothetical scenarios of situations that provided opportunities for sexual harassment if the men so chose. Instructions asked men to imagine themselves in these roles of the men and to consider what they would do in each situation. Men were then instructed to imagine that whatever their chosen course of action no negative consequences would result from their choices.

Results suggested that men who initiate severe sexually harassing behavior are likely to emphasize male social and sexual dominance, and to demonstrate insensitivity to other individuals' perspectives. Furthermore, men are less likely than women to define sexual harassment as including jokes, teasing remarks of a sexual nature, and unwanted suggestive looks or gestures. Men are also more likely than women to agree with the following statements, taken from M. A. Paludi's (1993) survey of "atttitudes toward victim blame and victim responsibility":

- Women often claim sexual harassment to protect their reputations.
- Many women claim sexual harassment if they have consented to sexual relations but have changed their minds afterwards.
- Sexually experienced women are not really damaged by sexual harassment.
- It would do some women good to be sexually harassed.
- Women put themselves in situations in which they are likely to be sexually harassed because they have an unconscious wish to be harassed.
- In most cases when a woman is sexually harassed, she deserved it.

Sexual harassment, similar to rape, incest, and battering, can be understood as an extreme acting-out of qualities that are regarded as super masculine in this culture: aggression, power, dominance, and force. Thus, men who harass exhibit stereotypic behaviors characteristic of the masculine gender role in American culture (Doyle and Paludi 1995). We will return to this perspective in chapters 3 and 4 when we discuss sexual harassment of students in elementary, secondary, and higher education.

Thus far our attention has been devoted to men as sexual harassers and women as recipients of the harassment. Do women sexually harass men in the workplace? It is possible for women to harass men. The incidence of this form of sexual harassment (female harasser, male victim) is small. The incidence of women sexually harassing other women is also small. Many of men's experiences with sexual harassment are with other men. Consquently, men are reluctant to disclose this information due to homophobic concerns (Levy and Paludi 1997). Research in this area of same-sex sexual harassment is still ongoing and we will offer more insight on this topic as well as suggestions for policies, procedures, and training programs.

THEORETICAL MODELS OF SEXUAL HARASSMENT

Sandra Tangri and her colleagues (Tangri, Burt, and Johnson 1982) have labeled three theoretical models that incorporate a gender/power/aggression analysis.

The *natural/biological model* interprets sexual harassment as a consequence of sexual interactions between people, either attributing men as "needing" to engage in aggressive sexual behavior, or describing sexual harassment as part of the "game" between sexual equals. This model does not account for the extreme stress reactions suffered by victims of sexual harassment.

The *sociocultural model* posits sexual harassment as only one manifestation of the much larger patriarchal system in which men are the dominant group. According to this model, sexual harassment is an example of men asserting their socially based personal power based on sex. This model gives a more accurate account of sexual harassment since the overwhelming majority of victims are women and the overwhelming majority of harassers are men.

The *organizational model* asserts that sexual harassment results from opportunities presented by organizational power. Since most workplaces are defined by power imbalances between supervisors and subordinates, individuals can use the power of their position to extort sexual gratification from their subordinates.

Related to this model is the research findings that suggest that individuals who harass typically do not label their behavior as sexual harassment despite the fact they report they frequently engage in behaviors that fit the legal definition of sexual harassment. They deny the inherent power differential between themselves and their employees.

The behavior that legally constitutes harassment is just that, despite what the supervisor's or coworker's intentions may be.

IMPACT OF SEXUAL HARASSMENT ON EMPLOYEES

Several reports documented the high cost of sexual harassment to women and to men who have been victimized. For example, Louise Fitzgerald and Alayne Omerod (1993) noted that the impact of sexual harassment can be examined from three main perspectives: work-related, psychological or emotional, and physiological or health-related.

Work-Related Outcomes. In the first Merit Systems study (1981), 10 percent of the women, who reported they were sexually harassed, reported changing jobs as a result. In the second study, Merit Systems (1987) noted that over thirty-six thousand federal employees left their jobs due to sexual harassment in the two-year period covered by their study. This incidence rate included individuals who quit, fired, transferred, or reassigned because of unwanted sexual attention. Additional research documented decreased morale and absenteeism, decreased job satisfaction, performance decrements, and damage to interpersonal relationships at work (Gutek and Koss 1993).

Psychological Outcomes. The consequences of harassment for employees' emotional well-being include: depression, helplessness, extreme sadness, strong fear reactions, loss of control, worry, disruption of their lives, and decreased motivation (Gutek and Koss 1993; Samoluk and Petty 1994).

Physiological Outcomes. The following physical symptoms have been reported in the literature concerning workplace sexual harassment: headaches, sleep disturbances, disordered eating, gastrointestinal disorders, nausea, weight loss or gain, and crying spells (Gutek and Koss 1993). Victims of sexual harassment can exhibit a "post abuse" syndrome characterized by shock, emotional numbing, constriction of affect, flashbacks, and other signs of anxiety and depression (Fitzgerald 1993; Salisbury, Ginoria, Remick, and Stringer 1986). These responses are influenced by disappointment in the way others react and by the stress of harassment-induced life changes such as moves, loss of income, and disrupted work history.

A study by the New York Division of Human Rights (1993) documented several direct costs women have experienced as a result of alleged sexual harassment, including: (*a*) legal expenses, (*b*) medical costs, and (*c*) psychotherapy costs. This study also reported the number of individuals who lost health benefits, life insurance, pensions, access to day care, or other benefits as a result of the alleged harassment.

Louise Fitzgerald, Y. Gold, and K. Brock (1990) classified individuals' responses into two categories: internally focused and externally focused strategies. Internal strategies represented attempts to manage the personal emotions and cognitions associated with the behaviors they experienced. As we discussed in chapter 1, Fitzgerald et al., identified the following classification system for internally focused strategies:

Detachment. Individual minimizes the situation, and treats it as a joke.

Denial. Individual denies behaviors; attempts to forget about it.

Relabeling. Individual reappraises the situation as less threatening, and offers excuses for the harasser's behavior.

Illusory Control. Individual attempts to take responsibility for the harassment.

Endurance. Individual puts up with behavior because she/he does not believe either help is available or fears retaliation.

Externally focused strategies focus on the harassing situation itself, including reporting the behavior to the individual charged with investigating complaints of sexual harassment. Fitzgerald, Gold, and Brock (1990) classified externally focused strategies into the following categories:

Avoidance. Individual attempts to avoid the situation by staying away from the harasser.

Assertion / Confrontation. Individual refuses sexual or social offers or verbally confronts the harasser.

Seeking Institutional / Organizational Relief. Individual reports the incident and files a complaint.

Social Support. Individual seeks support of others to validate perceptions of the behaviors.

Appeasement. Individual attempts to evade the harasser without confrontation, and attempts to placate the harasser.

Ormerod and Gold (1988), using this classification system, have noted that internal strategies represented by far the most common response overall. Most victims do not tell the harasser to stop. Their initial attempts to manage the initiator are rarely direct. Typically harassers are more powerful—physically and organizationally— than the victims, and sometimes the harasser's intentions are unclear. The first or first few harassing events are often ignored by victims—especially when they are experiencing hostile environment sexual harassment where the behavior may be more subtle. Victims may interpret or reinterpret the situation so that the incident is not defined as sexual harassment. Many times victims ignore the perpetrator.

Victims of sexual harassment may fear retaliation should they confront the harasser. The economic reality for most employees is that they can't just leave a workplace where they are being sexually harassed.

DEALING WITH SEXUAL HARASSMENT IN WORKPLACES

To deal effectively with sexual harassment in the workplace, we recommend the following components:

(a) an effective policy statement,
(b) an effective grievance procedure, and
(c) education/training programs for all members of the organization (Blaxall, Parsonson, and Robertson 1993; Howard 1991; Levy and Paludi 1997):

Policy Statement

In order to promote the effective and equitable resolution of problems involving sexual harassment, we recommend companies enforce an explicit policy (Connell 1991; Howard 1991; Levy and Paludi 1997). A policy allows the workplace to uphold and enforce its policies against sexual harassment within its own community (including such severe penalities as loss of pay or position) without requiring victimized individuals to undertake the laborious, protracted, and costly process of seeking redress from the courts. It also helps protect employers from incurring legal liability because they have failed to take steps to insure a workplace free of sexual harassment.

The components of an effective policy statement for corporations, as suggested by the courts (e.g., Robinson v. Jacksonville Shipyards), Equal Employment Opportunity Commission Policy Guidance, and human resource practice and research, are as follows (also see chapter 1):

- A statement of principles, specifying that sexual harassment is illegal and won't be tolerated.
- A definition of sexual harassment, including peer sexual harassment, and examples of behaviors that constitute sexual harassment.
- A statement outlining the impact of sexual harassment on employees and the workplace.
- Employees' responsibility to report sexual harassment.

- Organization's responsibility in responding to a report of sexual harassment.
- A statement concerning confidentiality.
- Description of the investigatory process.
- A statement concerning sanctions for sexual harassment, retaliation, and false complaints.
- An identification of individual(s) responsible for hearing complaints.
- An identification of the personnel services available to assist those with a complaint of sexual harassment (e.g, employees assistance program).

We also recommend the following:

1. The policy should be drafted in sex-neutral terms. These statements will enhance the acceptance of sexual harassment free environments by all employees.
2. The policy statement should contain an alternative procedure for complaints if the investigator is the alleged harasser.
3. The policy statement must be available in languages in addition to English.
4. The policy statement must be revised when new case law and state law modifications make it appropriate.
5. The policy statement must be reissued at least once a year and sent to all employees as well as posted throughout the workplace and in employee manuals. All new employees must be informed of the policy.

Investigatory Procedures

Procedures for investigating complaints of sexual harassment must take into account the psychological issues involved in the victimization process, including employees' feelings of powerlessness, isolation, changes in social network patterns, and a wish to gain control over their personal and professional lives. Supportive techniques for working with victims of sexual harassment include the following, adapted from Levy and Paludi (1997):

- Present the initial discussion as informal and informational.
- Acknowledge individuals' courage by stating how difficult it is to label, report, and discuss sexual harassment.
- Encourage individuals to share their feelings and perceptions.
- Provide information about the incidence of sexual harassment.
- Assure individuals that victims are not responsible for their victimization.
- Work with individuals in monitoring their physical, emotional, academic, and interpersonal responses to sexual harassment.
- Provide a safe forum for individuals' expressions of anger and resentment.
- Help individuals feel empowered.
- Suggest a peer counseling group for individuals who need support for dealing with their experiences.
- Work with individuals and organizations in their investigation of complaints of sexual harassment.

We recommend many of these same techniques for dealing with men and women who have been accused of sexual harassment:

- Acknowledge how difficult it is to be accused of sexual harassment.
- Encourage individuals to share their feelings and perceptions.
- Provide information about the incidence of sexual harassment.
- Work with individuals in monitoring their physical, emotional, academic, and interpersonal responses to being accused of sexual harassment.

- Provide a safe forum for individuals' expressions of anger and resentment.
- Suggest a peer counseling group for individuals who need support in dealing with their experiences.

Complainants and accused employees frequently exhibit the following responses:

- Confusion and/or embarrassment
- Helplessness
- Anger
- Anxiety
- Fear

We therefore recommend that the investigative process take into consideration these emotional responses to sexual harassment to assist the individual's path to recovery from the trauma of experiencing sexual harassment or being accused of sexual harassment. For example:

Accused's Response: Confusion
Investigator's Response: Help with labeling the experiences, and provide behavioral definitions of sexual harassment.
Complainant's Response: Helplessness
Investigator's Response: Discuss complainant's power in handling the case; focus on ways the individual is powerful in other aspects of her/his life.
Accused's Response: Anger
Investigator's Response: Discuss confidentiality of the investigative process; focus on ways to rebuild a career; offer support systems; validate the anger.
Complainant's Response: Worry
Investigator's Response: Discuss due process, sanctions against retaliation, and confidentiality of the investigative process.

Research has documented that the experience of participating in an investigative process can be as emotionally and physically stressful as the victimization itself. It is important not only to build in several support systems but also to help complainants and alleged harassers cope with the process of the complaint procedure. Investigators, who must make a determination whether to sustain the complaint, must not be counselors to either party in the complaint process. An employees assistance program may work with the investigator for this purpose.

Referrals to support groups and therapists in the community must be made readily available for all individuals involved in the investigatory procedure. It is important that the support group or counselor understand that their role is not to judge whether sexual harassment as legally defined has occurred. In addition, the support system is not an attorney. Counselors must only help individuals with their options, not advise them on their civil rights.

Support groups should allow individuals to express their anger by providing a safe forum for the expression of anger so that the individual can contain her/his feelings in the workplace and preserve an effective performance as much as possible. They should also provide for the individual who is mourning her/his losses. They need to be offered hope that their careers and relationships can be rebuilt. In chapter 1, we discuss the goals of support groups on sexual harassment.

Guidelines for Investigating
Complaints of Sexual Harassment

Businesses usually set up their own complaint procedure that fits their unique needs. However, the following general guidelines have been suggested for all investigations of sexual harassment (see Levy and Paludi 1997 for additional details):

- Investigators must state to all parties that the workplace *will not* ignore any complaint of sexual harassment.

- Every complaint must be kept confidential to protect the rights of all parties involved in the complaint.
- Investigators must not make determinations about the complaint based on the reputations of the individuals involved.
- The workplace's policy statement and procedures must be followed at all times.
- Every step of the investigation must be completely and accurately documented and in a form that can be defended to others.
- Investigations must be completed promptly.
- The complainant and accused must be interviewed in detail.
- Witnesses must be interviewed.
- All documents presented by the complainant, alleged harasser, and witnesses must be reviewed.
- Each complaint against the same individual must be handled independently.
- Closure must be provided for all parties involved in the complaint procedure.

Recordkeeping

A. Levy and M. A. Paludi (1997) recommend the following information be placed in the case file during the course of each investigation:

- Notes from meetings with complainant, alleged harasser, and witnesses.
- Letters from individuals involved in complaint procedures.
- Copies of all standard notification letters written to complainant and alleged harasser.
- Documents supplied by individuals involved in complaint procedure.

We recommend that all correspondence sent by the investigator (e.g., notification of charges of sexual harassment) be sent via certified mail. Home addresses must be used instead of work addresses.

Standard notification letters must be used with all complainants, witnesses, and alleged harassers.

The completed file should be given to the individual responsible for implementing sanctions with a copy of the formal report (i.e., CEO, for example, or the director of human resources).

Copies of the final report must never be given to any parties interviewed in the investigative process.

At the completion of the investigation, a letter to this effect must be sent from the investigator to the parties involved in the proceedings. A more formal letter will be sent to these individuals from the person responsible for sanctions. We recommend that the senior administrator send a letter of apology on behalf of the workplace to the complainant when her/his charges have been sustained.

It is recommended that records be kept for all procedures that are used, since without record keeping the workplace may deceive itself into believing that sexual harassment is a minor concern (Levy and Paludi 1997).

At the end of each year, the following information should be prepared for the CEO:

- The number of complaints filed by employees
- The number of complaints filed by managers
- The number of complaints that were sustained
- The number of complaints that were false
- The number of complaints for which insufficient information was present to sustain the charges
- The sanctions recommended by the investigator
- The sanctions adopted by the CEO
- Closure for all parties involved in all complaint procedures

Of course detailed information regarding the identities of the individuals involved in the complaint procedures should be omitted from newsletters. This technique will serve to highlight behaviors that constitute sexual harassment for the entire workplace as well as to indicate that sanctions would be administered for each case that is sustained, while maintaining confidentiality for individuals.

Remedial Action

Depending on the severity of sexual harassment complaint and findings of the investigator, the following options are available (Levy and Paludi 1997). These options can be recommended to the CEO by the investigator:

- **Verbal and/or written reprimands** concerning their behavior and warnings against any further sexual harassment. These reprimands must also make clear that further complaints will result in more severe sanctions, including dismissal.
- **Dismissal** when more severe sexual harassment has occurred. Collective bargaining agreements procedures must be followed.
- **Suspension without pay** may be an option when the recommendation involves counseling or other rehabilitative processes.
- **Transfers** for one or both individuals to other positions or courses within the workplace may be appropriate. This type of remedial action helps with potential retaliation and may also reduce stress for the person who has been harassed.
- **Demotions** of supervisory employees to non-supervisory positions.

We recommend contacting the complainant periodically for at least one year to determine whether the resolution of the complaint is satisfactory, whether any retaliation has occurred, and whether there has been any recurrence of the sexual harassment.

We also recommend periodically contacting the individual who has engaged in sexual harassment to determine whether there is any subsequent assistance the investigator can provide, for example, referrals for therapeutic support.

Finally, we recommend contacting the witnesses to determine whether they are experiencing any uncomfortableness or retaliatory behavior for their role in the investigation.

Training Programs

We believe the most important feature of an effective policy statement on sexual harassment is a training program designed to implement this policy. Effective training programs send a clear message to all individuals that the sexual harassment policy must be taken seriously and that sexual harassment will not be tolerated by management.

Goals for training programs should include the following:

1. To provide all members of the workplace with a clear understanding of their rights and responsibilities.
2. To enable individuals to distinguish between behavior that is sexual harassment and is not sexual harassment.
3. To provide individuals with information concerning the policy statement against sexual harassment and investigatory procedures set up by the organization.
4. To create an environment that is free of sexual harassment and free of the fear of retaliation for speaking out about sexual harassment.

Once goals have been established, the policy statement and investigatory procedures should be written (or revised) since they are part of the training session.

Psychological Impact of Participating in a Training Program on Sexual Harassment

Training programs on sexual harassment can pose difficulty for individuals: (*a*) the topic taps the painful or guilty experiences of many individuals; (b) resolutions of problems may seem out of reach and burdensome; and (c) employees may have to discuss situations in the presence of others directly involved in investigations. We recommend trainers respect these responses to training programs and build in time to address the concerns during the training session.

From our experience, questions that dominate the training sessions tend to be classified into two major types: those that deal with the nature of sexual harassment and abuse, and those that reflect frustration with the topic. Employees' questions often reflect fear and confusion surrounding sexual harassment. The topic of sexual harassment arouses discomfort and defensiveness. Joking is a common coping strategy individuals use in training sessions. An effective training session on sexual harassment should challenge gender stereotypes. Consequently, participants are going to be uncomfortable during the session.

It is important to give legitimacy to the anxieties, confusions, and fears raised by participants in the training programs. It is necessary to establish rapport and a respectful atmosphere. We also recommend talking straightforwardly about the attitudes individuals have brought with them to the session, perhaps using the issues raised in national media accounts of an example of sexual harasssment as a starting off point.

Some employees may be experiencing sexual harassment, and the anger they feel toward the perpetrator may be expressed toward the trainer. Therapeutic support staff (e.g, Employees Assistance Program personnel) must be present during training programs to assist in this regard. Furthermore, individuals may come to label their experiences as sexual harassment following their participation in the training session. It is therefore essential to have worked out investigatory procedures prior to the training program so that resolution of complaints can be dealt with immediately.

Guidelines for a Successful Training
Program on Sexual Harassment

First, all employess must be told in writing by the president and/or CEO to participate in the training program. All administrators must participate in the sessions as well. Employees' participation in a training session should be mandatory. Optional attendance at a training session conveys management's belief that sexual harassment is not an important enough topic to devote time to. And, inevitably, many of the employees who most need the sessions will avoid them. We recommend that the letter or memo be written in a straightforward, non-threatening manner, ensuring flexibility in accommodating work schedules. We suggest the CEO maintain a record of all employees who fail to participate in a training session. A letter to this effect should be placed in an employee's personnel file.

Second, all employees must receive resource material that summarizes the content of the training session. We recommend the following:

- Legal Definitions of Sexual Harassment
- Behavioral Definitions of Sexual Harassment
- Policy Statement Against Sexual Harassment
- Investigatory Procedures at the Organization
- Name and Phone Numbers/Office Numbers of Investigators
- Locations Where Information May be Obtained on Sexual Harassment
- Information Regarding Stress Effects of Sexual Harassment
- Referrals for Psychotherapeutic Support and Medical Help

Third, women and men must participate in the training program together. It is our experience that separate sessions for women and men may perpetuate stereotypes that all men are guilty of sexual harassment and all women are victims. This latter type of training is also divisive. Both women and men have the same rights and responsibilities with respect to sexual harassment, and they must be provided the same information concerning these rights and responsibilities.

Thus, sexual harassment training is not a lecture on what the law and company policy require. Sexual harassment training also requires dealing with individuals' assumptions and misconceptions about sexual harassment and their anxieties about the training itself. Training sessions must devote ample time to dealing with the participants' feelings, misconceptions, and questions (Levy and Paludi 1997). We recommend all sessions must be completed within a few weeks with a maximum of thirty to thirty-five individuals per training session so as to have ample discussion and contribution from all participants.

We offer resources for investigators and trainers in the next section.

RESOURCES FOR DEALING WITH SEXUAL HARASSMENT IN WORKPLACES

Training Program for Investigators of Complaints of Sexual Harassment

GOALS OF TRAINING PROGRAM

- Provide information on current laws relating to sexual harassment.
- Define quid pro quo and hostile environment sexual harassment.
- Discuss psychological issues involved in dealing with sexual harassment.
- Examine profiles of victims of sexual harassment.
- Discuss means of resolution for complaints of sexual harassment.

TOPICS FOR PRESENTATION AND DISCUSSION

Part 1   **Introduction to Training Session and Goals of Seminar/Workshop**

Part 2   **The Complainant's Perspective**

Part 3   **Psychology of the Victimization Process**

Part 4   **The Perspective of the Accused**

Part 5   **Differential Evaluations of Identical Behavior**

Part 6   **Keeping the Investigative Process Consistent with Responses**

BREAK

Part 7   **Interviewing Techniques**

Part 8   **Note-taking and Record Keeping**

Part 9   **Sample Case Studies**

Part 10 **Summary and General Discussion**

BREAK

Part 11 **Role Play Exercises**

"Train-the-Trainers" Workshop

CONTENT TRAINING

Topics for Presentation and Discussion

Part 1 Introduction to Training Session and Goals of Seminar/Workshop

- Trainer welcomes participants to seminar.
- Trainer introduces her/himself to participants and indicates:
  1. Responsibility in establishing a climate free of sexual harassment.
- Participants introduce themselves and state their goals for the training session.
- Trainer writes these goals on the flipchart/chalk-board for all participants to see.
- Trainer summarizes goals.
- Trainer lectures on the major components of the training session.

Part 2 Perceptions vs. Realities in Sexual Harassment

- Trainer uses case studies; asks participants to discuss them in small groups.
- Trainer summarizes individuals' responses to the case studies.
- Trainer makes summary comments from this unit.

Part 3 Definition of Sexual Harassment

- Trainer discusses the following issues with respect to the definition of sexual harassment:
  1. Quid pro quo and hostile environment sexual harassment
  2. Behavioral examples of sexual harassment
  3. Peer sexual harassment
  4. Examples of court cases

5. Selected issues, e.g., "reasonable woman" standard, "reasonable person" standard
• Trainer makes summary comments from this unit

Part 4 Incidence of Sexual Harassment

• National research studies
• Occupational group differences
• Distinction between incidence and reporting
• Underreporting of incidences
• Individuals at risk for sexual harassment
• Summary comments

BREAK

Part 5 Impact of Sexual Harassment on Individuals and Workplace

• Impact of sexual harassment on employees
• Work-related outcomes
• Physical outcomes
• Emotional outcomes
• Impact of sexual harassment on the workplace
• Summary comments

Part 6 Causes of Sexual Harassment

• Types of power bases
• Psychological profiles of harassers
• Summary comments

Part 7 Preventing Sexual Harassment in the Workplace

• Components of an effective policy statement
• Investigative procedures
• Summary comments

Part 8 Summary Comments and Review

• Trainer asks participants to reread case studies and discuss them in small groups.

- Trainer and participants discuss the responses to case studies.
- Trainer reviews participants' goals that were generated at the beginning of the session.
- Question and Answer Period.

BREAK

PEDAGOGY TRAINING

Topics for Presentation and Discussion

Part 1   Introduction to Pedagogy Training

Discussion of attitudes of employees in attending training sessions on sexual harassment

Part 2   Notifying Employees that They will Participate in Training Sessions

Part 3   Presenting Material on Sexual Harassment to Employees

BREAK

Part 4   Dealing with Anger, Frustration, and Anxiety on the Part of Employees Who Participate in Training Sessions

Part 5   How to Discuss Policy Statement and Grievance Procedures in Training Session

Part 6   Summary Comments and Review

Training Program on Sexual Harassment for Employees

CONTENT TRAINING

Topics for Presentation and Discussion

Part 1   Introduction to Training Session and Goals of Seminar

- Trainer welcomes participants to seminar.
- Trainer introduces her/himself, qualifications, background, and so forth.
- Trainer summarizes goals of seminar.
- Trainer asks each employee to state goal they have for the program.
- Trainer writes each response on flipchart/chalkboard for all participants to see.
- Trainer summarizes the goals of the participants in the training program.
- Trainer introduces sample case study; asks participants to get into small groups to discuss case study.

Case study is discussed throughout the rest of the sections:

Part 2   Definition of Sexual Harassment

- Summary of case law on quid pro quo and hostile environment sexual harassment.
- Behavioral examples of sexual harassment.
- Peer sexual harassment.
- Summary comments from this unit by trainer.

Part 3   Impact of Sexual Harassment on Individuals and Workplace Environment

- Trainer discusses the impact of sexual harassment on employees.
- Trainer discusses the cost of sexual harassment for the workplace.
- Trainer makes summary comments from this unit.

Part 4   Causes of Sexual Harassment

- Trainer highlights explanatory models of sexual harassment.
- Trainer discusses psychological profiles of harassers.
- Trainer summarizes comments from this unit.

Part 5   Preventing Sexual Harassment

- Trainer discusses the importance of policy statement, grievance procedures, and training.
- Trainer summarizes comments from this unit.
- Trainer distributes copies of policy statement and grievance procedures.
- Trainer introduces the individual who is responsible for investigating complaints.

Part 6   Summary Comments and Review

- Trainer summarizes major points from training program.
- Trainer leads general discussion of sexual harassment.
- General Question and Answer Period
- Individual Meetings with Interested Employees

Training Program on Effective Communication for Individuals Who Have Been Found to Have Violated Sexual Harassment Policies

OUTLINE OF TRAINING PROGRAM

Goals of Training Program

- Provide information concerning liability.
- Define quid pro quo and hostile environment sexual harassment.
- Discuss the interface of gender and power in the workplace.

- Discuss psychological issues involved in dealing with sexual harassment.
- Examine the physical and emotional reactions of being sexually harassed.
- Discuss peer sexual harassment.
- Review and learn effective verbal and nonverbal communication patterns.

Topics for Presentation and Discussion

Part 1 **Introduction to Training Session and Goals of Training**

Part 2 **What is Sexual Harassment?**
Legal Definitions
Behavioral Examples
Continuum of Sexual Harassment

Part 3 **Sexual Harassment *vs.* Flirtation and Compliments**

Part 4 **Hostile Environment and Gender Stereotyping**

Part 5 **Impact of Hostile Environment and Quid Pro Quo on Employees**

Part 6 **Impact of Hostile Environment and Quid Pro Quo on Workplace**

Part 7 **Intent *vs.* Impact**
Perspective Taking

Part 8 **Case Studies/Role Playing**

Part 9 **Policy Statement and Investigatory Procedures**

Part 10 **Review and General Discussion**

Part 11 **Discussion of "Homework" and Overview of Second Training Session**

Outline of Second Training Session

Part 1 **Introduction to Training Session and Goals of Training**

Part 2 **Review of "Homework" from First Session**

Part 3 **Role Playing/Case Studies on Sexual Harassment**

Part 4   Nonverbal Communication Patterns
          Types
          Eye Contact
          Touch
          Personal Space
          Body Posture
          Effective Communication in a Workplace
          Setting
          Dealing with Coworkers
          Dealing with Supervisors
Part 5   Verbal Communication Patterns
          Intent *vs*. Impact: How do Others Perceive
          One's Verbal Communication?
          "That's Not What I Meant."
          "You Don't Understand."
          Effective Verbal Communication in a Work-
          place Setting
Part 6   Behavioral Rehearsal: Role Playing What
          Was Discussed
Part 7   Resource Materials for Transfer of Training
Part 8   Review and General Discussion

Interviewing Techniques with Complainants and Accused Individuals

STATEMENTS ABOUT SEXUAL HARASSMENT EXPERIENCES

Example:

Individuals are unique in terms of how they respond to stress. However, there are some common symptoms shared by those who have experienced sexual harassment . . .

STATEMENTS DESIGNED TO GET CLARIFICATION

Examples:

"Let me see if I understand the situation you are describing. You are saying that . . ."

From your description of the incident it sounds like . . . Are you saying that it has been difficult to go to work as well as at home since you received word that a complaint has been filed against you?

Statements About Complaint Procedures

Example:

I can provide you with information about sexual harassment in general and our policy and procedures in particular.

Statements Concerning Referrals

Example:

If you would like to have the names and phone numbers of a support group or therapist, I will be pleased to provide you with that information.

We recommend consulting Levy and Paludi (1997) for additional interviewing techniques.

Educational Qualifications of Trainers

We recommend that trainers be interviewed in person by a few individuals who represent the group of individuals for whom the training will be provided. Areas of inquiry include:

1. Education/training in the psychological issues involved in sexual harassment
2. Education/training in the legal issues involved in this area
3. Publications/presentations on the topic
4. List of previous training seminars/workshops and individuals who can give recommendations about previous training programs
5. Outlines and/or video tapes of previous training seminars/workshops

6. Familiarity with companies of the size of the present one
7. Ability to work with administrators, including human resource specialists
8. Education/training in psychological issues involved in facilitating a training program

REFERENCES

Baker, Nancy. 1989. "Sexual Harassment and Job Satisfaction in Traditional and Nontraditional Industrial Occupations." Ph.D. diss., California School of Professional Psychology, Los Angeles.

Blaxall, M., B. Parsonson, and N. Robertson. 1993. "The Development and Evaluation of a Sexual Harassment Contact Person Training Package." *Behavior Modification* 17: 148–163.

Connell, D. 1991. "Effective Sexual Harassment Policies: Unexpected Lessons From Jacksonville Shipyards." *Employee Relations* 17: 191–206.

Doyle, J., and M. A. Paludi. 1995. *Sex and Gender: The Human Experience*. 3rd ed. Dubuque: Wm. C. Brown.

Fitzgerald, Louise F. 1993. "Sexual Harassment: Violence Against Women in the Workplace." *American Psychologist* 48: 1070–1076.

Fitzgerald, L. F., Y. Gold, and K. Brock. 1990. "Responses to Victimization: Validation of an Objective Policy." *Journal of College Student Personnel* 27: 34–39.

Fitzgerald, L. F., and Alayne Ormerod. 1993. "Sexual Harassment in Academia and the Workplace." In *Psychology of Women: A Handbook of Issues and Theories*. Edited by F. Denmark and M. A. Paludi. Westport, CT: Greenwood Press.

Fitzgerald, L. F., S. Shullman, N. Bailey, M. Richards, J. Swecker, A. Gold, A. Ormerod, and L. Weitzman. 1988. "The Incidence and Dimensions of Sexual Harassment in Academia and the Workplace." *Journal of Vocational Behavior* 32: 152–175.

Fitzgerald, L. F., and L. Weitzman. 1990. "Men Who Harass: Speculation and Data. In *Ivory Power: Sexual Harassment on Campus*. Edited by M. A. Paludi. Albany: State University of New York Press.

Gold, Y. August 1987. "The Sexualization of the Workplace: Sexual Harassment of Pink-, White- and Blue-collar Workers." Paper presented to the annual conference of the American Psychological Association in New York.

Gutek, Barbara. 1985. *Sex and the Workplace*. San Francisco: Jossey-Bass.

Gutek, Barbara, and M. Koss. 1993. "Changed Women and Changed Organizations: Consequences of and Coping with Sexual Harassment. *Journal of Vocational Behavior* 42: 28–48.

Howard, S. 1991. "Organizational Resources for Addressing Sexual Harassment. *Journal of Counseling and Development* 69: 507–511.

LaFontaine, E., and L. Tredeau. 1986. "The Frequency, Sources, and Correlates of Sexual Harassment Among Women in Traditional Male Occupations. *Sex Roles* 15: 423–432.

Levy, A., and M. A. Paludi. 1997. *Workplace Sexual Harassment*. Englewood Cliffs, NJ: Prentice Hall.

Lott, B. 1990. "The Perils and Promise of Studying Sexist Discrimination in Face-to-Face Situations. In *Ivory Power: Sexual Harassment on Campus*. Edited by M. A. Paludi. Albany: State University of New York Press.

New York Division of Human Rights. 1993. "Survey of the Costs of Sexual Harassment." Reported in J. Avner, Chairperson, *Sexual Harassment: Building a Consensus for Change*. Final Report Submitted to Governor Mario Cuomo, Albany, NY.

Ormerod, Alayne and Y. Gold. March 1988. "Coping with Sexual Harassment: Internal and External Strategies for Coping with Stress." Paper presented to the annual conference of the Association for Women in Psychology, Bethesda, MD.

Paludi, M. A. October 1993. "Sexual Harassment in Corporate America." Paper presented at the Columbia Conference on Sexual Harassment, New York, NY.

Pryor, John. 1987. Sexual Harassment Proclivities in Men. *Sex Roles* 17: 269–290.

Salisbury, J., A. Ginoria, H. Remick, and D. Stringer. 1986. "Counseling Victims of Sexual Harassment." *Psychotherapy* 23: 316–324.

Samoluk, S., and G. Petty. 1994. "The Impact of Sexual Harassment Simulations on Women's Thoughts and Feelings." *Sex Roles* 30: 679–699.

Tangri, Sandra, M. Burt, and L. Johnson. 1982. Sexual Harassment at Work: Three Explanatory Models. *Journal of Social Issues* 38: 33–54.

U.S. Merit Systems Protection Board. 1981. "Sexual Harassment of Federal Workers: Is it a Problem?" Washington, DC: U.S. Government Printing Office.

———. 1987. "Sexual Harassment of Federal Workers: An Update." Washington, DC: U.S. Government Printing Office.

Zalk, S. 1996. "Psychological Profiles of Men Who Harass." In *Ivory Power: Sexual Harassment on Campus*. Edited by M. A. Paludi. Albany: State University of New York Press.

CHAPTER 3

Sexual Harassment on College Campuses

**INCIDENCE OF SEXUAL HARASSMENT
ON COLLEGE CAMPUSES**

Dziech and Weiner (1984) reported that 30 percent of undergraduate women suffer sexual harassment from at least one of their instructors during four years of college. When definitions of sexual harassment include sexist remarks and other forms of "gender harassment," the incidence rate in undergraduate populations nears 70 percent (Paludi 1996).

Research by Adams, Kottke, and Padgitt (1983) reported that 13 percent of the women they surveyed said they had avoided taking a class or working with a particular professor because of the risk of being subjected to sexual advances. In this same study, 17 percent of the women reported verbal sexual advances, 14 percent received sexual invitations, 6 percent had been subjected to physical advances, and 2 percent reported direct sexual bribes.

Similar results were obtained with graduate women students by Bailey and Richards (1985). They reported that 13 percent of 246 women graduate students in their sample indicated they had been sexually harassed, 21 percent had not enrolled in a course to avoid such behavior, and 16 percent indicated they had been directly assaulted.

M. Bond (1988) reported that 75 percent of the 229 women who responded to her survey experienced offensive jokes with sexual themes during their graduate training, 69 percent were subjected to sexist comments demeaning to women, and 58 percent of the women reported experiencing sexist remarks about their clothing, body, or sexual activities. Fitzgerald, Shullman, Bailey, Richards, Swecker, Gold, Ormerod, and Weitzman (1988) investigated approximately two thousand women at two major state universities. Half of the women respondents reported experiencing some form of sexually harassing behavior. The majority of this group reported sexist comments directed toward them by faculty; the next largest category of harassment behavior was seductive behavior, including faculty who invited them for drinks and a backrub, or brushed up against them, or showed up uninvited to their hotel rooms during out-of-town academic conferences or conventions.

Research by Paludi, DeFour, and Roberts (1994) suggests that the incidence of academic sexual harassment of ethnic minority women is even greater than that reported by white women. Dziech and Weiner (1984) and DeFour (1996) suggest that ethnic minority women are more vulnerable to receiving sexual attention from professors. Ethnic minority women are subject to stereotypes about sex, are viewed as sexually mysterious and inviting, and are less sure of themselves in their careers (DeFour 1996). Although all students are vulnerable to some degree, male teachers and faculty tend to select those who appear most vulnerable and defenseless. Thus, for certain student groups, the incidence of sexual harassment appears to be higher than others (Barickman, Paludi, and Rabinowitz 1992). For example:

- Women of color, especially those with "token" status.
- Graduate students, whose future careers are often determined by their association with a particular faculty member.

- Students in small colleges or small academic departments, where the number of faculty available to students is quite small.
- Women students in male-populated fields, e.g., engineering.
- Students who are economically disadvantaged and work part-time or full-time while attending classes.
- Lesbian women, who may be harassed as part of homophobia.
- Physically or emotionally disabled students.
- Women students who work in dormitories as resident assistants.
- Women who have been sexually abused.
- Inexperienced, unassertive, socially isolated girls and women, who may appear more vulnerable and appealing to those who would intimidate or entice them into an exploitive relationship.

As Fitzgerald and Omerod (1993) conclude:

. . . it seems reasonable (if not conservative) to estimate that one out of every two women will be harassed at some point during her academic or working life, thus indicating that sexual harassment is the most widespread of all forms of sexual victimization studied to date. (p. 559)

IMPACT OF SEXUAL HARASSMENT ON COLLEGE STUDENTS

Several reports have documented the high cost of sexual harassment to individuals (Koss 1990; Quina 1990; Rabinowitz 1996). Similar to the results with employees (see chapter 2), research with college students suggests that there are career-related, psychological, and physiological outcomes of sexual harassment. For example, women students have reported decreased morale, decreased satisfaction with their career goals, and lowered grades. In addition, women students have reported feelings of helplessness and powerlessness over their academic lives, strong fear reactions, and decreased motivation. Women students have also reported headaches, sleep disturbances, eating disorders, and gastrointestinal disorders as common physical responses to sexual harassment.

These responses are influenced by disappointment and self-blame in the way others react and the stress of sexual harassment-induced life changes, such as loss of student loans, loss of teaching or research fellowships, and disrupted educational history. For example, 29 percent of the women in Schneider's (1987) research reported a loss of academic or professional opportunities, and 14 percent reported lowered grades or financial support, because of sexual harassment.

CONSENSUAL RELATIONSHIPS

Neither Title IX nor Title VII prohibit consensual sexual relationships between faculty and students; however, a number of institutions are developing policies on this matter. While consensual relationships may not always be unethical, they almost always cause problems. This happens, according to Sandler and Paludi (1993) for the following reasons:

- The situation involves one person exerting power over another.
- The seduction of a much younger individual is usually involved.
- Conflict of interest issues arise. For example, how can a teacher fairly grade a student with whom he/she is having a sexual relationship?
- The potential for exploitation and abuse is high.
- The potential for retaliatory harassment is high when the sexual relationship ceases.
- Other individuals may be affected and claim favoritism.

M. C. Stites (1996) noted how including consensual relationships as part of the definition of academic sexual harassment has been met with considerable resistance. There are a few campuses (e.g., University of Iowa, Harvard University, Temple University) that prohibit sexual relationships between faculty and students over whom the professor has some authority (i.e., advising, supervising, grading, teaching). A few other campuses have "discouragement policies," in which "consensual relations" are not strictly prohibited but discouraged (e.g., University of Minnesota, University of Connecticut, New York University Law School, Massachusetts Institute of Technology). The University of Virgina called for a total ban on all sexual relationships between faculty and students regardless of the professor's role vis-à-vis the student. However, the Faculty Senate has approved a prohibition-only policy rather than the total ban policy. Thus, this campus prohibits sexual relations between faculty and students when the faculty has some organizational power over the student. The case can be made, however, that a faculty member does not have to be the student's professor in order for that faculty member to be powerful and potentially abuse that power over the student.

All faculty members have an ethical and professional responsibility to provide a learning environment that is respectful of students and fosters the academic performance and intellectual development of students.

It is our opinion that the fact that a student is defined as an adult by chronological age can in no way remove the obligation of a teacher or administrator to refrain from engaging in sexual harassment, and the student's adulthood is in no way a proxy for consenting to a relationship. A faculty member's relationship with a student (as a mentor, for example) can often involve emotional complexities and power differentials similar to the relationship of a counselor/therapist and a client.

The stories women tell about their consensual relationships do not parallel romances or typical stories about sexual affairs; instead they resemble stories depicting patterns of manipulation and victimization, responses identical to those women who are sexually harassed in a nonconsensual relationship (Zalk, Paludi, and Dederich 1991). DeChiara (1988) argues that students will be spared the stress of coping with unwanted sexual attention from professors when a college has a consensual relationship policy. And Keller (1990) suggests that when a college does not address consensual relationships in their sexual harassment policy, professors can:

> disguise sexually harassing behavior as academic or personal attention . . . and students have no way of knowing whether or not they can fairly categorize a faculty member's behavior as harassment. A single request for a date, for example, unaccompanied by a threat of retaliation or the promise of gain, may not constitute sexual harassment under certain policies that focus on more intimidating and coercive behavior. (pp. 30–31)

WHO HARASSES?

Most individuals believe that sexual harassers in the academy and the workplace are pathological, abnormal, and easily spotted. L. F. Fitzgerald and L. Weitzman (1990) have reported, following their study of men on college/university faculties, that the stereotype that there is a "typical" harasser who can be identified by his blatant and obvious mistreatment of many women is a serious oversimplification of a complex issue and contributes to the misunderstanding of this issue. Harassers are found in all teaching ranks and exhibit many kinds of harassing behaviors. Fitzgerald and Weitzman also have noted that it may be painful to confront the reality that harassment can be perpetrated by teachers who are familiar to students, who have traditional family lives, and who appear to be caring and sensitive to their students.

Individuals who harass typically do not label their

behavior as sexual harassment despite the fact they report they frequently engage in intiating personal relationships with individuals. They deny the inherent power differential between themselves and their students as well as the psychological power conferred by this differential that is as least as salient as the power derived from their role as evaluators (Levy and Paludi 1997; Paludi 1996).

Kenig and Ryan (1986) indicate that male professors are less likely than female professors to define sexual harassment as including jokes, teasing remarks of a sexual nature, and unwanted suggestive looks or gestures. In addition, female professors are more likely than men to disapprove of romantic relationships between students and faculty. Male professors are also more likely than female professors to agree with the following statements: "An attractive woman has to expect sexual advances and learn how to handle them"; "It is only natural for a man to make sexual advances to a woman he finds attractive"; and "People who receive annoying sexual attention usually have provoked it."

Kenig and Ryan also have reported that male professors are more likely than female professors to believe individuals can handle unwanted sexual attention on their own without involving the college or university. Thus, male professors view sexual harassment as a personal, not an organizational issue. They attribute more responsibility to women victims of sexual harassment and minimize the responsibility of the college administration.

Bernice Lott (1993) and her colleagues also have found empirical support for a widely accepted assumption among researchers in sexual harassment that sexual harassment is part of a larger and more general misogyny. This hostility toward women includes extreme stereotypes of women such as the idea that sexual harassment is a form of seduction that women secretly need/want to be forced into sex (see chapters 2 and 4 for additional discussions of this issue).

B. Dziech and L. Weiner (1984) have classified academic sexual harassers in two categories: public and private. Public harassers are professors who engage in flagrant sexist and/or seductive behavior toward women students. Private harassers are restrained, intimidating professors who coerce students with their formal authority. In addition to these two categories, Dziech and Weiner suggest other roles that may be assumed by a professor who sexually harasses students: counselor/helper, confidant, intellectual seducer, and opportunist. The intellectual seducer requires self-disclosure on the part of students (e.g., through journal writing), which he then uses to gain personal information about the student. The opportunist uses the physical setting (e.g., a laboratory) to gain intimacy with students.

Sue Rosenberg Zalk (1990) acknowledges, however, that the "bottom line" in the relationship between professors and students is power:

> The faculty member has it and the student does not. As intertwined as the faculty-student roles may be, and as much as one must exist for the other to exist, they are not equal collaborators. The student does not negotiate—indeed, has nothing to negotiate with. (p. 145)

She further argues that professors' greatest power lies in their capacity to:

> . . . enhance or diminish students' self-esteem. This power can motivate students to master material or convince them to give up. It is not simply a grade, but the feedback and the tone and content of the interaction. Is the student encouraged or put down? Does the faculty member use his/her knowledge to let students know how "stupid" they are or to challenge their thinking? This is real power. (p. 146)

STUDENT RESPONSES TO SEXUAL HARASSMENT

This power differential that exists between students and professors helps to explain students' desire to remain quiet about their experiences with sexual harassment. Research involving students' experiences with sexual harassment suggest that they are similar to employees: First, most students do not tell the harasser to stop. And their initial attempts to manage the initiator are rarely direct. Typically harassers are more powerful—physically and institutionally—than students, and sometimes the harasser's intentions are unclear and the harasser has authority, status, and power (similar to rapists).

The first or first several harassing events are often ignored by victims—especially when they are experiencing hostile environment sexual harassment where the behavior is more subtle. Students may interpret or reinterpret the situation so that the incident is not defined as sexual harassment. Many times victims ignore the perpetrator.

As we discussed in Chapter 2, Fitzgerald, Gold, and Brock (1990) have constructed an empirically based system for classifying individuals' responses to sexually harassing behaviors. They have divided individuals' responses into two categories: internally focused strategies and externally focused strategies. Internal strategies represent attempts to manage the emotions and cognitions associated with the behaviors they have experienced. For example, students who use internally focused strategies typically deny the event or relabel it so as not to appear a victim.

Students fear retaliation should they confront the harasser. Students do not want their careers threatened. As Sandler and Paludi (1993) argued, most students are serious about school; they do not enjoy experiencing sexual harassment. Malovich and Stake (1990) found that women students who were high in performance self-esteem and held nontraditional gender role attitudes were more likely to report incidents of sexual harassment than women who were high in self-esteem and who held traditional gender role attitudes, or women who were low in self-esteem. Brooks and Perot (1991) found that reporting behavior was predicted by the severity of the offense and by feminist attitudes on the part of the student. Reilly, Lott, and Gallogly's (1986) study of college students reported that 61

percent of women victims ignored the behavior or did nothing, and 16 percent asked or told the faculty member to
stop.

IMPLICATIONS FOR EDUCATION AND POLICY

With respect to sexual harassment of college students,
we can make the following summary statements:

1. Sexual harassment does not fall within the range
   of personal private relationships. It happens when
   a professor with power abuses that power to intimidate, coerce, or humiliate a student because of
   their sex;
2. Sexual harassment is a breach of the trust that
   normally exists among professors and students;
3. Sexual harassment creates confusion because the
   boundary between professional roles and personal
   relationships is blurred. The harasser introduces a
   sexual element into what should be a professional
   situation;
4. Students often do not label their experiences as
   sexual harassment despite the fact that their experiences meet the legal definition of sexual harassment;
5. Professors often deny the power inherent in their
   position in the college hierarchy;
6. Sexual harassment on campus often goes unre-
   ported because students fear retaliation should
   they deal with the harassment directly;
7. The impact of sexual harassment on students is
   enormous and impairs their emotional and physical health as well as their career development and
   commitment.

To deal effectively with sexual harassment in schools
and colleges/universities, we recommend the following
resources, which take into account these above-mentioned

seven issues: (1) an effective policy statement, (2) an effective investigative procedure, and (3) education/training
programs for all members of the educational institution.
We offer resources, as we did in Chapter 2, for each of these
components in the following section. Resources presented
in other chapters may be adapted for use with college students.

RESOURCES FOR DEALING WITH SEXUAL HARASSMENT ON COLLEGE CAMPUSES

Seminar on Sexual Harassment
for College Students

GOALS OF TRAINING PROGRAM

- Define quid pro quo and hostile environment sexual harassment.
- Discuss psychological issues involved in dealing with sexual harassment.
- Discuss the physical and emotional reactions to being sexually harassed.
- Provide a psychological profile of sexual harassers.
- Discuss peer sexual harassment.
- Discuss means of resolving complaints of sexual harassment.

OBJECTIVES OF TRAINING PROGRAM

At the conclusion of this training program, students will be able to:

- Assess their own perceptions of the definition, incidence, and psychological dimensions of sexual harassment.
- Label adequately behaviors as illustrative of sexual harassment or not illustrative of sexual harassment.
- Assess why students choose to report or not report their experiences of sexual harassment.
- Identify peer sexual harassment.
- Identify students' rights and responsibilities under Title IX.
- Understand the college's policy statement against sexual harassment and investigatory procedures for dealing with sexual harassment.
- Design educational programs for their campus to deal with sexual harassment, including peer sexual harassment.

- Understand resources available for students who are sexually harassed.

Topics for Presentation and Discussion

Part 1   Introduction to Training Session and Goals of Seminar

- Students state their goals for the training session.
- Facilitator writes these goals on the flipchart/chalkboard for all students to see.
- Facilitator summarizes goals of participants.
- Facilitator lectures on the major goals of the training session.

Part 2   Perceptions vs. Realities in Sexual Harassment: Students' Views of Sexual Harassment

- Facilitator distributes copies of sexual harassment case study.
- Facilitator asks students to work in small groups to discuss case studies.
- Facilitator posts students' responses on the flipchart/ chalkboard.
- Facilitator lectures on the similarities between the exercise/case and issues to be discussed on sexual harassment.
  a. Sexual harassment is illegal;
  b. A variety of responses exists for individuals dealing with sexual harassment;
  c. Professors' power over students makes students modify their behavior for fear of retaliation.
- Facilitator makes summary comments for this unit.

Part 3   Definition of Sexual Harassment

- Facilitator lectures and leads guided discussion of sexual harassment.

    a. Equal Employment Opportunity Commission and Office of Civil Rights definitions
    b. Summary of case law on quid pro quo and hostile environment sexual harassment
    c. Behavioral examples of sexual harassment
    d. Peer sexual harassment
- Facilitator makes summary comments from this unit.

Part 4   Incidence of Sexual Harassment Among College Students

- Facilitator lectures on the incidence of academic sexual harassment.
    a. Measurement considerations
    b. Underreporting of incidences
    c. Individuals at risk for sexual harassment
    d. Relationship between incidence and reporting
- Facilitator makes summary comments from this unit.

Part 5   Impact of Sexual Harassment on Students and Campus

- Facilitator lectures on the impact of sexual harassment on students.
- Facilitator lectures on the cost of sexual harassment for the college/university.
- Facilitator makes summary comments from this unit.

Part 6   Causes of Sexual Harassment

- Facilitator lectures on explanatory models of sexual harassment.
- Facilitator lectures on psychological profiles of harassers.
- Facilitator makes summary comments from this unit.

Part 7   Preventing Sexual Harassment on Campus

- Facilitator lectures on components of an effective policy statement for students.
- Facilitator distributes copies of college's policy statement against sexual harassment.
- Facilitator introduces college representative charged with enforcing policy statement.
- Facilitator discusses policy statement.
- Facilitator asks students to list potential educational programs for their college/university campus.
- Facilitator writes these responses on the flipchart/ chalkboard for all students to see.
- Facilitator makes summary comments from this unit.

Part 8   Summary Comments and Review

- Facilitator lectures on "myths and realities" of sexual harassment.
- Facilitator leads general discussion of sexual harassment of college students.
- Facilitator asks students to reread case study and answer questions.
- Facilitator reviews students' goals that were generated at the beginning of the session.
- Question and Answer Period

Sample Case Studies

Jamie is taking a laboratory course in psychology in her third semester at college. She is having a rather difficult time conducting one experiment and using statistics to analyze her results She decides to talk with the graduate teaching assistant for the course about her work. While she is discussing the research, her teaching assistant suggests that the two of them date. Jamie makes it quite clear that she isn't interested in him romantically. Throughout the remainder of the semester, Jamie receives low grades on her research papers. When she asks her teaching assistant about his grading system, he replies, "You had your chance."

Discussion

1. Does the behavior outlined in this case study seem inappropriate to you? Why or why not?
2. Do you believe the behavior described in the case study illustrates sexual harassment? Why or why not?
3. If you believe this is sexual harassment, what kind of sexual harassment do you believe this case study illustrates?
4. How do you think the individuals involved feel? Are they scared? upset? angry? embarassed? guilty?
5. Do you believe there is miscommunication between the individuals in the case study? Were there mixed messages and crossed signals?
6. What do you think the individuals should do?
7. If you observed this situation occurring, what, if anything, would you do? Why?
8. What services would be available at your campus to assist with the situations described?
9. If you were the student in this case study, what services would you want, if any, to assist you?
10. Do you belive the sex or sexual orientation of the individuals in the case study make any difference in your evaluation of the situation?
11. Do the individuals involved in the case study have a responsibility (moral, professional, legal, or otherwise) to behave differently? Explain.
12. What outcome would you like to see in this case? Explain.
13. Is discussing the case difficult? Why or why not?

At a department meeting, Professor Helmsley, the Director of Graduate Studies, expresses his opinion that undergraduate courses in literature offered under the Women's Studies Program are useless as preparation for graduate study. He therefore recommends that they be dropped from the list of acceptable courses for the undergraduate major in literature.

Discussion

1. Is this sexual harassment? Why or why not?
2. If Professor Helmsley expressed a similar opinion during a lecture to his undergraduate class, would he be engaging in a form of sexual harassment?

In her introductory pychology class, Sonia, a Latina, notices that her professor smiles and comments on her appearance as a greeting each morning—and that he does not greet any other student in this way. Before his lecture on contemporary sexual roles and behavior, he remarks to the class, "Sonia can probably help us understand this topic since she has to put up with macho types."

Discussion

1. Is this sexual harassment? Why or why not?
2. If you think harassment has occurred, is all of the professor's behavior harassing?

Kevin is taking an introductory English course. His first writing assignment deals with his uncertainties about being a new student in college, on his own for the first time. When the essays are returned, his has no grade and only the comment, "Please see me." Kevin goes to his teacher's office during the posted office hours. His teacher suggests that they go out for a drink to discuss the essay.

Discussion

1. Is this sexual harassment? Why or why not?
2. Does it matter whether Kevin's teacher is a man or a woman? . . . a professor, high school teacher, college adjunct or teaching assistant?

Maria is taking a course dealing with human physiology this semester. Her professor has been discussing anatomy and today brings in slides to complement his lecture. For twenty-five minutes the class sits through a discussion of male anatomy, complete with slides from Gray's Anatomy textbook. Following this presentation and class discussion, Maria's professor begins to lecture on female anatomy. He explains that for lack of time he will show only a few select slides that illustrate the points he wants to make about female anatomy. Maria at once notices that the slides are nude photos from men's magazines.

Discussion

1. Do you think this illustrates sexual harassment? Why or why not?
2. What should Maria do?

Connie is taking a math course that includes a unit on statistics. She knows that this course is important to her career and a good grade in math can increase her chances of getting into graduate school. Connie has been having some difficulty in understanding probability theory. She decides to talk with her professor about this topic. She tells him about her concern about the material and her wish to get a good grade because she wants to go to graduate school. Connie's professor makes it clear that all she has to do is to become sexually involved with him.

Discussion

1. Do you think this illustrates sexual harassment? Why or why not?
2. What should Connie do?

Teaching Techniques

- Ask students to share their ideas about why there is an underreporting of incidents of sexual harassment on campus.
- Show a videotape or film about sexual harassment. Ask students whether the reenactments adequately portray the emotional and physical impact of being sexually harassed.
- Ask students to describe resources available on their campus for dealing with academic sexual harassment. Invite the individual(s) responsible for handling complaints and/or educating the campus community about sexual harassment to visit your class.
- Provide students with a copy of the campus' policy statements and procedures. Discuss the procedures available for students. Ask students to indicate how the campus handles issues of confidentiality, due process, and timely resolution of cases.
- Ask students to design a two-hour workshop on academic sexual harassment, including reference to peer harassment, for a first year student orientation program.
- Ask students to comment on the "silent language" of the classroom. Topics to include: eye contact, nodding and gesturing, posture, modulating tone. Have students keep a week-long log of nonverbal behavior on the part of students in their classes. Ask students to note gender similarities and differences.

- Review recent case law in hostile environment and quid pro quo sexual harassment. Set up a mock courtroom trial to reenact the cases discussed.
- Invite a therapist who specializes in treating victims of sexual harassment to discuss treatment approaches.
- Ask students to list behaviors they believe illustrate "flirting." Then ask students to indicate how they feel when they are flirting and when they are the recipient of flirtatious behavior.
- Have students distinguish between sexual harassment and flirting.
- Distribute copies of statements referring to individuals' attitudes toward victim blame and victim responsibility. For example:
  a. Women often claim sexual harassment to protect their reputations.
  b. Any woman may be sexually harassed.
  c. Many women claim sexual harassment if they have consented to sexual relations but have changed their minds afterwards.
  d. A woman should not blame herself for sexual harassment.
  e. Sexually experienced women are not really damaged by sexual harassment.
  f. Many women invent sexual harassment stories if they learn they are failing a course.
  g. It would do some women good to be sexually harassed.
  h. Women do not provoke sexual harassment by their appearance or behavior.
  i. Women put themselves in situations in which they are likely to be sexually harassed because they have an unconscious wish to be harassed.
  j. Men can be sexually harassed too.
- Ask students to discuss their responses to these statements. Cite research evidence for each statement.

Educating the Campus Community
About Peer Sexual Harassment

- Include the policy against peer harassment in the policy statement on sexual harassment.
- Peer harassment policies need to apply to race, disability, sexual orientation, in addition to sex.
- Include information about academic sexual harassment, including reference to peer harassment in faculty and student orientation materials.
- Hold a Peer Harassment Awareness Week and schedule programs around the issue of lesbian and gay harassment.
- Mention peer harassment in speeches to reinforce its importance as an institutional priority.
- Require that student leaders attend workshops on peer harassment.
- Encourage sororities and fraternities to present programs on peer harassment.
- Include information on sexual harassment, including peer harassment, in packets for transfer students.
- Report annually on sexual harassment, including peer harassment.
- Encourage faculty to incorporate discussions of sexual harassment, including peer harassment, in their courses.

Campus Checklist for Sexual Harassment

- Are there policies and effective procedures for dealing with academic sexual harassment? with workplace sexual harassment?
- Do the policies forbid peer harassment behaviors or are they limited to harassment by faculty, administrators, and other staff?
- Are remedies clear and commensurate with the level of violation?

- Are the policies forbidding sexual harassment well publicized? Are they circulated periodically among students, staff, faculty, and administrators?
- How do individuals in your campus community learn whom they should see to discuss sexual harassment?
- Are there specific individuals to whom individuals can go for help with sexual harassment issues?
- Does your campus have procedures to inform new faculty, staff, and students about sexual harassment?
- Does your campus have a task force or other structure that examines and reports annually on sexual harassment?
- Is there a panel or other group which has the responsibility for educating the campus community about sexual harassment?
- Are there regular campus workshops on sexual harassment, including peer harassment?
- What services are available to individuals who have experienced sexual harassment?

Discussing Sexual Harassment
in the College Curriculum

MATHEMATICS/STATISTICS

- Methodology used to obtain incidence rates of sexual harassment.
- Scaling of scenarios depicting sexual harssment.
- Reliability and validity issues in incidence surveys.

PSYCHOLOGY/SOCIOLOGY

- Interaction of gender, race, and power in faculty-student relationships.
- Attitudes toward victim blame and victim responsibility.

POLITICAL SCIENCE
- Social and public policy applications of research on sexual harassment.
- Legal issues in sexual harassment.

HEALTH/COUNSELING
- Symptoms associated with sexual harassment victimization.
- Therapeutic interventions with victims of sexual harassment.

HISTORY
- Sexual harassment of employed women from an historical perspective.
- Development of policies and procedures for dealing with sexual harassment.

Seminar on Sexual Harassment for Faculty

GOALS OF TRAINING PROGRAM

- Provide information concerning liability.
- Discuss legal requirements and mandates.
- Define quid pro quo and hostile environment sexual harassment.
- Discuss psychological issues involved in dealing with sexual harassment.
- Consider the physical and emotional reactions to being sexually harassed.
- Provide a psychological profile of sexual harassers.
- Discuss peer sexual harassment.
- Discuss means of resolving complaints of sexual harassment.

OBJECTIVES OF TRAINING PROGRAM

At the conclusion of this training program, faculty will be able to:

1. Assess their own perceptions of the definition, incidence, and psychological dimensions of sexual harassment.
2. Label adequately behaviors as illustrative of sexual harassment or not illustrative of sexual harassment.
3. Assess why individuals choose to report or not report sexual harassment.
4. Identify peer sexual harassment.
5. Identify students' and employees' rights and responsibilities under Title IX and Title VII.
6. Design educational programs for their campus to deal with sexual harassment, including peer sexual harassment.
7. Understand how they can create a classroom atmosphere that will discourage sexual harassment.

TOPICS FOR PRESENTATION AND DISCUSSION

Definition of Sexual Harassment

- Summary of case law on quid pro quo and hostile environment sexual harassment
- Behavioral examples of sexual harassment
- Peer sexual harassment

Incidence of Sexual Harassment

- Measurement considerations
- Underreporting of incidences
- Individuals at risk for sexual harassment
- Relationship between incidence and reporting

Impact of Sexual Harassment on Individuals and Campus

- Sexual Harassment Trauma Syndrome
- Internal and external coping styles

BREAK

Causes of Sexual Harassment

- Explanatory models of sexual harassment
- Organizational power
- Sociocultural power
- Psychological profiles of harassers

Preventing Sexual Harassment on Campus

- Establishing policies and procedures for dealing with sexual harassment
- Techniques for classroom use
- Campus-wide educational programs

Summary Comments and Review

- "Myths and Realities" of sexual harassment
- Question and answer period

Suggestions for Graduate Teaching Assistants

- Behavior rules for the outside, voluntary social environment do not always apply in the involuntary college environment where people are a "captive audience"and where an instructor has substantial power over students.
- Teaching Assistants who communicate their clear stand against sexual harassment help prevent incidents of sexual harassment.
- Sexual harassment is not an expression of sexual interest. It is an abuse of power and a form of control.
- Changing an organizational culture from one that encourages sexual harassment to one that prohibits and punishes it takes the burden away from individuals and lessens the organization's exposure to charges.

- Graduate Teaching Assistants are viewed as resource people—individuals to consult when students need advice on issues relating to sexual harassment. Often they are closer to students in age and experience than full-time faculty.

Seminar for Training Faculty Trainers
Time for Training Program: 8 Hours

CONTENT TRAINING

Goals of Training

- Provide information concerning liability.
- Provide information about current law relevent to sexual harassment.
- Define quid pro quo and hostile environment sexual harassment.
- Discuss psychological issues involved in dealing with sexual harassment.
- Consider the physical and emotional reactions to being sexually harassed.
- Provide a psychological profile of sexual harassers.
- Discuss peer sexual harassment.
- Discuss means of resolving for complaints of sexual harassment.

Objectives of Training Program

At the conclusion of this training program, trainers will be able to:

- Assess their own perceptions of the definition, incidence, and psychological dimensions of sexual harassment;
- Distinguish behavior that is sexual harassment from behavior that is not;
- Assess why individuals choose to report or not report sexual harassment;

- Identify peer sexual harassment;
- Identify students' and employees' rights and responsibilities under Title IX and Title VII;
- Design educational programs for their campus to deal with sexual harassment, including peer sexual harassment.

Topics for Presentation and Discussion

Part 1   Introduction to Training Session and Goals of Seminar/Workshop
(20 minutes)

- Trainer welcomes participants to seminar.
- Trainer introduces her/him self to participants and indicates the importance of faculty and administrators' responsibility in establishing a climate free of sexual harassment.
- Participants introduce themselves and state their goals for the training session.
- Trainer writes these goals on the flipchart/chalkboard for all participants to see.
- Trainer summarizes goals.
- Trainer lectures on the major components of the training session.

Part 2   Perceptions vs. Realities in Sexual Harassment
(20 minutes)

- Trainer uses case studies and asks participants to discuss them in small groups.
- Trainer summarizes individuals' responses to questions concerning sexual harassment.
- Trainer makes summary comments from this unit.

Part 3   Definition of Sexual Harassment
(30 minutes)

- Trainer lectures and leads guided discussion of sexual harassment.

1. Summary of case law on quid pro quo and hostile environment sexual harassment
2. Behavioral examples of sexual harassment
3. Peer sexual harassment
- Trainer makes summary comments from this unit.

Part 4   Incidence of Sexual Harassment
(20 minutes)

- Trainer lectures on the incidence of workplace sexual harassment.
- Trainer lectures on the incidence of academic sexual harassment.
  1. Measurement considerations
  2. Underreporting of incidences
  3. Individuals at risk for sexual harassment
  4. Relationship between incidence and reporting
- Trainer makes summary comments from this unit.

BREAK—10 minutes

Part 5   Impact of Sexual Harassment on Individuals and Campus
(25 minutes)

- Trainer lectures on the impact of sexual harassment on employees.
- Trainer lectures on the impact of sexual harassment on students.
- Trainer lectures on the cost of sexual harassment for the college/university.
- Trainer makes summary comments from this unit.

Part 6   Causes of Sexual Harassment
(20 minutes)

- Trainer lectures on explanatory models of sexual harassment.
- Trainer lectures on psychological profiles of harassers.
- Trainer makes summary comments from this unit.

Part 7   Preventing Sexual Harassment on Campus
   (45 minutes)

- Trainer leads small group discussions about prevention of sexual harassment on campus.
- Trainer lectures on the components of an effective policy statement for employees.
- Trainer identifies pedagogical techniques for classroom discussions.
- Trainer asks participants to list additional educational programs for their college/university campus.
- Trainer makes summary comments form this unit.

Part 8   Summary Comments and Review
   (30 minutes)

- Trainer lectures on "myths and realities" of sexual harassment.
- Trainer leads general discussion of sexual harassment.
- Trainer asks participants to reread case study and answer questions.
- Trainer reviews participants' goals that were generated at the beginning of the session.
- Question and Answer Period

LUNCH BREAK—1 1/2 Hours

PEDAGOGY TRAINING

Goals of Training

- Provide information concerning creating an atmosphere conducive to training faculty.
- Discuss use of role playing, case studies, scenarios in training faculty.
- Discuss use of pre-training and post-training surveys.

Objectives of Training Program

At the conclusion of this training program, trainers will be able to:

- Assess their own perceptions of their ability to provide training for faculty.
- Address adequately questions concerning content.
- Administer surveys to assess attitudes and prevalence regarding sexual harassment.
- Design educational programs for their campus to deal with sexual harassment, including peer sexual harassment.

Topics for Presentation and Discussion

Part 1   Introduction to Pedagogy Training
(20 minutes)

- Discussion of attitudes of faculty in attending training sessions on sexual harassment.
- Discussion of ways to empower faculty who are participating in sexual harassment training.
- Trainer summarizes goals.

Part 2   Notifying Faculty that They will Participate in Training Sessions
(20 minutes)

Part 3   Presenting Material on Sexual Harassment to Faculty
(60 minutes)

- Definitions of sexual harassment.
- Impact of sexual harassment on individuals and campus.
- Effective verbal and nonverbal communication strategies.
- Explanatory models of sexual harassment.

BREAK—10 minutes

Part 4   Dealing with Anger, Frustration, and Anxiety on the Part of Faculty Participating in Training Sessions
(60 minutes)

Part 5　How to Discuss Policy Statement and Investigatory Procedures in Training Session
(30 minutes)

Part 6　Summary Comments and Review
(30 minutes)

Sample Policy Statement Against Sexual Harassment on College Campuses

Members of an academic community must be able to work in an atmosphere of mutual respect and trust. Any violation of trust, any form of intimidation or exploitation, damages the college's integrity by undermining the essential freedoms of inquiry and expression.

As a place of studying and work, —— College should be free of sexual harassment and all forms of sexual intimidation and exploitation. All individuals must be assured that —— College will take action to prevent such misconduct and that anyone who engages in such behavior may be subject to disciplinary procedures.

It is therefore the Policy of —— College that all individuals have a right to work and learn in an environment free of sexual harassment. —— College strongly disapproves of sexual harassment of its members in any form. All individuals at all levels must avoid sexually harassing behavior and will be held responsible for insuring that the campus is free from sexual harassment.

WHAT IS SEXUAL HARASSMENT?

Sexual harassment is legally defined as "unwelcome sexual advances, requests for sexual favors, and other verbal or physical conduct of a sexual nature" when any one of the following criteria is met:

- Submission to such conduct is made either explicitly or implicitly a term or condition of the individual's employment or academic standing;
- Submission to or rejection of such conduct by an individual is used as the basis for employment or academic decisions affecting the individual;
- Such conduct has the purpose or effect of unreasonably interfering with an individual's work or academic performance or creating an intimidating, hostile, or offensive work or learning environment.

Examples of the legal definition of sexual harassment include, but are not limited to:

- Unwelcome sexual advances
- Request for sexual favors, whether or not accompanied by promises or threats with regard to the professional relationship
- Sexually degrading words to describe an individual
- Sexually suggestive objects, books, magazines, posters, photographs, cartoons, or pictures

These behaviors constitute sexual harassment whether they are committed by individuals who are in a supervisory positions or by peers. And, these behaviors constitute sexual harassment if they occur between individuals of the same sex or between individuals of the opposite sex. —— College prohibits these and other forms of sexual harassment.

COSTS OF SEXUAL HARASSMENT

Sexual harassment causes high costs to individuals. The outcomes of sexual harassment can be examined from three main perspectives: learning/work-related, emotional, and health-related.

Learning / Work-Related Outcomes. Research has documented that decreased morale and absenteeism, decreased job satisfaction and performance, and damage to interpersonal relationships with colleagues frequently occurs because of sexual harassment.

Emotional Outcomes. The consequences of being harassed are devastating to the emotional health of individuals. It often causes depression, helplessness, strong fear reactions, loss of control, disruption of lives, and decreased motivation.

Health Outcomes. The following physical symptoms have been reported by individuals who have been sexually harassed: headaches, sleep disturbances, disordered eating, gastrointestinal disorders, nausea, weight loss or gain, and crying spells.

Sexual harassment is not a welcomed behavior; it is unwanted, unwelcomed, and interferes with an individual's ability to get his/her work or studying accomplished.

WHAT SHOULD INDIVIDUALS DO IF THEY BELIEVE THEY ARE BEING SEXUALLY HARASSED?

Members of the —— Campus community, who have complaints of sexual harassment by anyone on campus, including any supervisors, faculty, or students, are encouraged to report such conduct to the —— officer so that he/she may investigate and resolve the problem.

The —— officer will give advice and guidance on both formal and informal procedures for resolving the problem. She/he will make a record of the contact, but all information will be kept confidential.

Individuals who feel subjected to sexual harassment should report the circumstances in writing within 60 days to the —— officer.

Individuals covered by collective bargaining agreements should feel free to be accompanied by their union representative in any and all meetings with the —— officer regarding a sexual harassment complaint.

Complainants and those against whom complaints have been filed will not be expected to meet together to discuss the resolution of the complaint unless the complainant requests this procedure.

Resolutions of Informal Complaints

Any individual may discuss an informal complaint with the —— officer. If the person who discusses an informal complaint is not willing to be identified to the person against whom the informal complaint is being made, the —— officer will make not only a confidential record of the circumstances, but also will provide guidance about various ways to resolve the problem or avoid future occurrences.

If the person bringing the complaint is willing to be identified to the person against whom the complaint is made and wishes to attempt informal resolution of the problem, the —— officer will make a confidential record of the circumstances (signed by the complainant)and suggest and/or undertake appropriate discussions with the person involved.When a number of people report incidents of sexual harassment that have occurred in a public context (e.g., offensive sexual remarks in a classroom setting or an office) or when the —— administrator receives repeated complaints from different people that an individual has engaged in other forms of sexual harassment, the person complained against will be informed without revealing the identity of the complainants. The —— officer will suggest appropriate counseling or educational forums.

Resolutions of Formal Complaints

A formal complaint of sexual harassment must include a written statement signed by the complainant specifying the incident(s) of sexual harassment. The statement may be prepared by the complainant as a record of the complaint.

The complaint must be addressed to the —— officer, who will then investigate the complaint, and present his/her findings and recommendations to the president.

Formal complaints will be investigated in the following manner:

The —— officer will inform the person complained against of the name of the person making the complaint as well as of the substance of the complaint. The investigation will be limited to what is necessary to resolve the complaint or make a recommendation. If it appears necessary for the —— officer to speak to any people other than those involved in the complaint, he/she will do so only after informing the complaining person and the person complained against.

The —— officer will endeavor to investigate all complaints of sexual harassment expeditiously and professionally. To the extent possible, the investigation will be completed within thirty days from the time the formal investigation is initiated.

The —— will also make every attempt to maintain the information provided to them in the complaint and investigation process as confidentially as possible.

—— College's first priority will be to attempt to resolve the problem through a mutual agreement of the complainant and the person complained against.

If an individual making a formal complaint asks not to be identified until a later date (for example, until the completion of a course or a performance appraisal), the —— officer will decide whether or not to hold the complaint without further action until the date requested.

If a formal complaint has been preceded by an informal investigation, the —— officer shall decide whether there are sufficient grounds to warrant a formal investigation.

After an investigation of a complaint, the —— officer will report his/her findings with appropriate recommendations for corrective action to the president or report to the president its finding that there is insufficient evidence to support the complaint.

Following receipt of the report, the president may take such further action as he/she deems necessary, including the initiation of disciplinary proceedings.

RECOMMENDED CORRECTIVE ACTION

The purpose of any recommended corrective action to resolve a complaint will be to correct or to remedy the injury, if any, to the complainant and to prevent further harassment. Recommended action may include: written or oral reprimand of the harasser, suspension, dismissal, or transfer of the harasser, or other appropriate action.

If the complainant is not satisfied with the attempts to resolve the sexual harassment, the claimant may seek resolution through other sources, for example, the —— State Division of Human Rights, the United States Equal Employment Opportunity Commission, or the State Education Department.

RETALIATION

There will be no retaliation against individuals for reporting sexual harassment or assisting the —— officer in the investigation of a complaint. Any retaliation against an individual is subject to disciplinary action.

FALSE COMPLAINTS

If after investigating any complaint of sexual harassment it is discovered that the complaint is not bona fide or that an individual has provided false information regarding the complaint, the individual may be subject to disciplinary action.

Remember:

- **Sexual harassment is illegal.**
- **Sexual harassment is prohibited at —— College.**
- **Sexual harassment is not flirtation; it is unwelcomed behavior.**

- **Complimenting an individual is not sexual harassment.**
- **Sexual harassment may result in disciplinary action up to and including dismissal.**
- **Sexual harassment is harmful to all individuals involved and to the effective functioning of the campus.**
- **Retaliation for filing a sexual harassment complaint is prohibited and is subject to disciplinary action.**
- **—— College is committed to dealing with sexual harassment in an effective, confidential, and caring manner.**

For additional information regarding sexual harassment, contact:

These individuals have received training in the legal and psychological issues involved in sexual harassment.

Examples of College
Consensual Relationship Policies

PROHIBITION POLICY

At _____ College, no faculty member will have an amorous relationship with a student who is enrolled in a course being taught by the faculty member or whose work is being supervised by the faculty member.

DISCOURAGEMENT POLICY

At _____ College, amorous relationships between faculty and students are deemed very unwise, although not expressly forbidden. We recommend against such relationships when the professor has a direct authority over the student. If any college-related problems develop from such a relationship, the faculty member is entirely responsible.

TOTAL-BAN POLICY

At _____ College, no amorous relationship between faculty and students will be tolerated. This policy extends to faculty who are not teaching, advising, or supervising a student currently.

POTENTIAL CONFLICT OF INTEREST POLICY

At _____ College, we recognize that faculty-student relationships are asymmetric in nature. Therefore, amorous relationships between faculty and students can lead to difficulties. In such relationships, the faculty member faces serious conflicts of interest and must distance her/himself from any academic decisions involving the student. Failure to do so will constitute a violation of an ethical obligation to the student and to the College.

REFERENCES

Adams, J., J. Kottke, and J. Padgitt. 1983. "Sexual Harassment of University Students." *Journal of College Student Personnel* 24: 484–490.

Bailey, N., and M. Richards. August 1985. "Tarnishing the Ivory Tower: Sexual Harassment in Graduate Training Programs." Paper presented at the Annual Meeting of the American Psychological Association, Los Angeles, California.

Barickman, R. B., M. A. Paludi, and V. C. Rabinowitz. 1992. "Sexual Harassment of Students: Victims of the College Experience." In *Victimization: An International Perspective.* Edited by E. Viano. New York: Springer.

Bond, M. 1988. "Division 27 Sexual Harassment Survey: Definition, Impact, and Environmental Context." *The Community Psychologist* 21: 7–10.

Brooks, L., and A. Perot. 1991. "Reporting Sexual Harassment: Exploring a Predictive Model." *Psychology of Women Quarterly* 15: 31–47.

DeChiara, P. 1988. "The Need for Universities to Have Rules on Consensual Relationships Between Faculty and Students." *Columbia Journal of Law and Social Problems* 21: 137–162.

DeFour, D. C. 1996. "The Interface of Racism and Sexism on College Campuses." In *Ivory Power: Sexual Harassment on Campus*. Edited by M. A. Paludi. Albany: State University of New York Press.

Dziech, B., and L. Weiner. 1984. *The Lecherous Professor.* Boston: Beacon Press.

Fitzgerald, L. F., Y. Gold, and K. Brock. 1990. Responses to Victimization: Validation of an Objective Policy. *Journal of College Student Personnel* 27: 34–39.

Fitzgerald, L. F., and A. Omerod. 1993. "Sexual Harassment in Academia and the Workplace." In *Psychology of Women: Handbook of Issues and Theories*. Edited by F. L. Denmark and M. A. Paludi. Westport, CT: Greenwood.

Fitzgerald, L. F., S. Shullman, N. Bailey, M. Richards, J. Swecker, Y. Gold, A. Omerod, and L. Weitzman. 1988. "The Incidence and Dimensions of Sexual Harassment in Academia and the Workplace." *Journal of Vocational Behavior* 32: 152–175.

Fitzgerald, L. F., and L. Weitzman. 1990. "Men Who Harass: Speculation and Data." In *Ivory Power: Sexual Harassment on Campus*. Edited by M. A. Paludi. Albany: State University of New York Press.

Keller, E. 1990. "Consensual Relationships and Institutional Policy." *Academe* 76: 29–32.

Kenig, S., and J. Ryan. 1986. "Sex Differences in Levels of Tolerance and Attribution of Blame for Sexual Harassment on a University Campus. *Sex Roles* 15: 535–549.

Koss, M. P. 1990. "Changed Lives: The Psychological Impact of Sexual Harassment." In *Ivory Power: Sexual Harassment on Campus*. Edited by M. A. Paludi. Albany: State University of New York Press.

Levy, A., and M. Paludi. 1997. *Workplace Sexual Harassment.* Edgewood Cliffs, NJ: Prentice Hall.

Lott, B. 1993. "Sexual Harassment: Consequences and Realities. *NEA Higher Education Journal* 8: 89–103.

Malovich, N. J., and J. E. Stake. 1990. "Sexual Harassment of Women on Campus: Individual Differences in Attitude and Belief." *Psychology of Women Quarterly* 14: 63–81.

Paludi, M. A., ed. 1990. *Ivory Power: Sexual Harassment on Campus.* Albany: State University of New York Press.

―――. 1996. *Sexual Harassment on College Campuses: Abusing the Ivory Power.* Albany: State University of New York Press.

Paludi, M. A., D. C. DeFour, and R. Roberts. 1994. *Academic Sexual Harassment of Ethnic Minority Women.* Research in progress.

Project on the Status and Education of Women. 1978. *Sexual Harassment: A Hidden Issue.* Washington, DC: Association of American Colleges.

Quina, K. 1996. "The Victimizations of Women." In *Ivory Power: Sexual Harassment on Campus.* Edited by M. A. Paludi. Albany: State University of New York Press.

Rabinowitz, V. C. 1996. "Coping with Sexual Harassment." In *Ivory Power: Sexual Harassment on Campus.* Edited by M. A. Paludi. Albany: State University of New York Press.

Reilly, M., B. Lott, and S. Gallogly. 1986. Sexual Harassment of University Students. *Sex Roles* 15: 333–358.

Sandler, B., and M. A. Paludi. 1993. *Educator's Guide to Controlling Sexual Harassment.* Washington: Thompson.

Schneider, B. 1987. "Graduate Women, Sexual Harassment, and University Policy. *Journal of Higher Education* 58: 46–65.

Stites, M. C. 1996. Consensual Relationships. In *Sexual Harassment on College Campuses: Abusing the Ivory Power.* Edited by M. A. Paludi. Albany: State University of New York Press.

Zalk, S. R. 1996. "Men in the Academy: A Psychological Profile of Harassment. In *Ivory Power: Sexual Harassment on Campus*. Edited by M. A. Paludi. Albany: State University of New York Press.

Zalk, S. R., M. A. Paludi, and J. Dederich. 1991. "Women Students' Assessment of Consensual Relationships with Their Professors: Ivory Power Reconsidered. In *Academic and Workplace Sexual Harassment: A Resource Manual*. Edited by M. A. Paludi and R. B. Barickman. Albany: State University of New York Press.

CHAPTER 4

Sexual Harassment in K–12

INCIDENCE

In 1993, the American Association of University Women collected incidence rates of adolescents' experiences with sexual harassment. In this first national study of sexual harassment of adolescents, 1,632 students in grades 8 through 11 from 79 schools across the United States were asked: "During your whole school life, how often, if at all, has anyone (this includes students, teachers, other school employees, or anyone else) done the following things to you when you did not want them to?"

- Made sexual comments, jokes, gestures, or looks.
- Showed, gave, or left you sexual pictures, photographs, illustrations, messages, or notes.
- Wrote sexual messages/graffiti about you on bathroom walls, in locker rooms, etc.
- Spread sexual rumors about you.
- Said you were gay or lesbian.
- Spied on you as you dressed or showered at school.
- Flashed or "mooned" you.
- Touched, grabbed, or pinched you in a sexual way.
- Pulled at your clothing in a sexual way.
- Intentionally brushed against you in a sexual way.

- Pulled your clothing off or down.
- Blocked your way or cornered you in a sexual way.
- Forced you to kiss him/her.
- Forced you to do something sexual, other than kissing.

Results suggested that four out of five students (81 percent) reported that they have been the target of some form of sexual harassment during their school lives. With respect to gender comparisons, 85 percent of girls and 76 percent of boys surveyed reported they experienced unwelcomed sexual behavior that interfered with their ability to concentrate at school and with their personal lives.

The AAUW study also analyzed for race comparisons. African American boys (81 percent) were more likely to have experienced sexual harassment than white boys (75 percent) and Latinos (69 percent). For girls, 87 percent of whites reported having experienced behaviors that constitute sexual harassment, compared with 84 percent of African American girls and 82 percent of Latinas.

The AAUW study also suggested that adolescents' experiences with sexual harassment are most likely to occur in the middle school/junior high school years (6th to 9th grade). The behaviors reported by students, in rank order from most experienced to least experienced is the following:

Sexual comments, jokes, gestures, or looks	(76% of girls; 56% of boys)
Touched, grabbed, or pinched in a sexual way	(65% of girls; 42% of boys)
Intentionally brushed against in a sexual way	(57% of girls; 36% of boys)
Flashed or "mooned"	(49% of girls; 41% of boys)
Had spread sexual rumors about them	(42% of girls; 34% of boys)
Had clothing pulled at in a sexual way	(38% of girls; 28% of boys)

Shown, given, or left sexual pictures, photographs, illustrations, messages, or notes	(31% of girls; 31% of girls)
Had their way blocked or cornered in a sexual way	(38% of girls; 17% of boys)
Had sexual messages/graffiti written about them on bathroom walls, in locker rooms, etc.	(20% of girls; 18% of boys)
Forced to kiss someone	(23% of girls; 14% of boys)
Called gay or lesbian	(10% of girls; 23% of boys)
Had clothing pulled off or down	(16% of girls; 16% of boys)
Forced to do something sexual, other than kissing	(13% of girls; 9% of boys)
Spied on as they dressed or showered at school	(7% of girls; 7% of boys)

Thus, similar to college students and employees, adolescents most frequently experienced hostile environment sexual harassment from peers. Students reported that they experience these behaviors while in the classroom or in the hallways as they were going to class. And the majority of harassment in schools was student-to-student (i.e., peer harassment). However, 25 percent of harassed girls and 10 percent of boys reported being harassed by teachers or other school employees. Unlike most research studies of adults, however, the incidence of reported sexual harassment of boys nearly equaled the sexual harassment of girls.

A number of research studies subsequent to the AAUW report reinforced the AAUW findings. For example, Bruce Roscoe and his colleagues (1994) reported a significant percentage of early adolescents' experiences with sexual harassment by peers. In a sample of 561 teens' experiences with sexual harassment, Roscoe found that 50 percent of the girls and 37 percent of the boys had been victimized. Adolescents also indicated that their tolerance of sexual harassment was quite low.

Similar results were obtained by Penelope Turner (1995), who administered a sexual harassment questionnaire to 201 students in grades 6, 7, and 8. Turner's results suggested that girls were more sensitive to verbal and physically harassing behaviors than boys. As a final example, K. Corbett (1993) conducted a retrospective study of 185 college students concerning their experiences with sexual harassment in high school. Her results suggested that half of the women and men cited incidents of peer sexual harassment.

Karen Bogart and her colleagues (Bogart, Simons, Stein, and Tomaszewski 1992) reviewed the sexual harassment complaints brought by students against teachers to the Massachusetts Department of Education. Among the complaints they reported were the following:

A science teacher measured the craniums of the boys in the class and the chests of the girls. The lesson in skeletal frame measurements were conducted one by one, at the front of the class, by the teacher.

The print shop teacher, who was in the habit of putting his arms around the shoulders of the young women, insisted, when one young woman asked to be excused to go to the nurse to fix her broken pants' zipper, that she first show him her broken zipper. She was forced to lift her shirt to reveal her broken pants' zipper. (p. 197)

Girls in nontraditional high school programs have reported the following experiences (Stein, 1986, cited in Bogart, Simmons, Stein, and Tomaszewski, 1992):

One female in diesel shop refused to go to lunch during her last two years of shop because she was the only young woman in the lunchroom at that time. When she went to the cafeteria, she was pinched and slapped on the way in, and had to endure explicit propositions made to her while she ate lunch.

A particular shop's predominantly male population designated one shop day as National Sexual Harassment Day, in honor of their only female student. They gave her non-stop harassment throughout the day, and found it to be so successful (the female student was forced to be dismissed during the day), that they later held a National Sexual Harassment Week. (p. 208)

These accounts provide a better picture than do simple percentages of the types of behaviors children and adolescents are experiencing at school. Adolescents are more likely to experience teacher/student sexual harassment and student/student sexual harassment if they attend schools which, according to Bernice Sandler and Michele Paludi (1993):

- Do not have a policy prohibiting sexual harassment.
- Do not disseminate the policy or report information regarding sexual harassment.
- Do not have a training program for teachers, staff, and students.
- Do not intervene officially when sexual harassment occurs.
- Do not support sexual harassment victims.
- Do not remove sexual graffiti quickly.
- Do not sanction individuals who engage in sexual harassment.
- Do not inform the school community about the sanctions for offenders.
- Have been previously an all-male school, or have a majority of male students.

WHY ADOLESCENTS SEXUALLY HARASS

Paludi (1993) has noted in her research on why boys and men sexually harass girls and women that the focus should not be on males' attitudes toward females but on males' attitudes toward other males, competition, and power. Many of the men with whom Paludi has discussed sexual harassment often act out of extreme competitiveness, ego, or fear of losing their positions of power. They don't want to appear weak or less masculine in the eyes of other males so they engage in the "scoping of girls," pinching girls, making implied or overt threats, or spying on women. Girls and women are the objects of the game to impress other boys and men. When boys are encouraged to be obsessionally competitive and concerned with dominance, it is likely that they will eventually use violent means to achieve dominance (Paludi 1993). Paludi also has noted that boys are also likely to be abusive verbally and intimidating in their body language. De-individuation is common among adolescent boys who, during class changes and lunchbreak, scope girls as they walk by in the hall. These boys discontinue self-evaluation and adopt group norms and attitudes. Under these circumstances, group members behave more aggressively than they would as individuals.

The elements of aggression so deeply embedded in the masculine gender role inevitably manifest themselves in sexual harassment. For many boys (and men), aggression is one of the major ways of proving their masculinity, especially among those men who feel some sense of powerlessness in their lives (Doyle and Paludi 1995). The male-as-dominant or male-as-aggressor is a theme so central to many adolescent males' self-concept that it literally carries over into their interpersonal communications, especially with female peers. Sexualizing a professional relationship may be one area where a man can still prove his masculinity when few other areas can be found for him to prove himself in control, or the dominant one in a relationship. Thus, sexual harassment is not so much a deviant act as an over-conforming act to the masculine role in this culture (Paludi 1996).

Greta Shilling Phinney (1994) also has reported that sexual harassment is a "dynamic element" in the lives of adolescent girls since schools perpetuate this male dominance through pedagogical techniques and sports. And, according to Elizabeth Chamberlain (1994):

> Sexual harassment is a manifestation of the ubiquitous power imbalance between men and women that is an essential part of the institution of compulsory heterosexuality. Any and all attempts, by laws, policies, or educational programs to eradicate sexual harassment will remain largely necessary but not sufficient until the root cause, power imbalance, is recognized.

Nan Stein (1994) has argued that sexual harassment, especially peer sexual harassment, is rampant in elementary and secondary schools; it is usually tolerated and characterized as "normal." Stein reminds us that regardless of the ways school administrators interpret sexual harassment, it does violate Title IX of the Education Amendments and it interferes with students' right to receive equal educational opportunities.

IMPACT OF SEXUAL HARASSMENT ON ADOLESCENTS

The AAUW (1994) study reported that approximately one in four students, who had been sexually harassed, did not want to attend school or cut a class. In addition, one in four students became silent in their classes following their experience of sexual harassment. With respect to the emotional aspects of sexual harassment, the AAUW study reported the following experiences, in rank order, among the students who were sexually harassed:

- Embarassment
- Self-consciousness
- Being less sure of themselves or less confident
- Feeling afraid or scared
- Doubting whether they could have a happy romantic relationship

• Feeling confused about who they are
• Feeling less popular

Sexual harassment victims may experience a second victimization when they attempt to deal with the situation through legal and/or institutional means. Stereotypes about sexual harassment and victimization blame girls and women for the harassment. These stereotypes center on the myths that sexual harassment is a form of seduction, that girls and women secretly want to be sexually harassed, and that they do not tell the truth (Stein 1986, cited in Bogart, Simmons, Stein, and Tomaszewski 1992).

Students may not label their experiences as sexual harassment, despite the fact their experiences meet the legal definition of this form of victimization. Consequently they may not label their stress-related responses as being caused or exascerbated by the sexual harassment. Their responses can be attributed by peers, teachers, and family to other events in their life—biological and/or social.

The responses of the trauma syndrome are influenced by disappointment in the way others react, for example, the stress of harassment-induced life changes such as moves and disrupted school history (Paludi 1996). Students and their families may also have to incur legal expenses, medical costs, and psychotherapy costs.

Stein (1993) suggests that another impact of sexual harassment is that it teaches girls to accept assault. She argues that this is especially the case when school administrators do not deal with the abuse.

HOW ADOLESCENTS COPE WITH SEXUAL HARASSMENT

The AAUW (1994) study reported that fewer than one in ten students who had been sexually harassed told a teacher, although girls were twice as likely to report their experiences as boys. In addition, fewer than one in four students who had been sexually harassed told a family member about their experiences. The majority of adolescents reported their experiences told a friend. Still, a size-able number of students remained silent about sexual harassment.

As research suggested (e.g., Fitzgerald and Omerod 1993; Paludi 1990), students fear retaliation should they confront the harasser. Students do not want their school careers or reputations threatened. Malovich and Stake (1990) found that women students, who were high in per-formance self-esteem and who held nontraditional gender role attitudes, were more likely to report incidents of sex-ual harassment than women who were high in self-esteem and who held traditional gender role attitudes, or women who were low in self-esteem. Brooks and Perot (1991) reported similar results.

PREVENTING SEXUAL HARASSMENT OF CHILDREN AND ADOLESCENTS: THE NEED FOR TRAINING PROGRAMS

It is important that the school's policy statement and investigatory procedures be communicated to all students as well as teachers and non-teaching employees. Elemen-tary and secondary schools students must know their rights and responsibilities with respect to being a com-plainant, an accused, and a witness. As we stated in our chapters on workplace and college sexual harassment, the most effective way to communicate the grievance proce-dure and policy statement is through training programs.

Bruce Roscoe and his colleagues (1994) reported that following a training program for seventh and eighth graders at a public middle school, reports of sexual harassment increased. In addition, 85 percent of the girls and 73 percent of the boys indicated the training was valuable with respect to understanding definitions, impact, and resolution.

Suggestions for Training Programs with Children and Adolescents

Cognitive Maturity. Children's and adolescents' level of cog-nitive development must be taken into consideration. For example, prior to adolescence, children need to be provided with concrete examples, not hypothetical, theoretical situations, in order for them to accurately grasp a concept. Thus, permitting children to watch a videotape of peer harassment, and depicting children the same age as the viewers, would be a helpful tool in the curriculum training program. We also recommend behavioral rehearsal or role playing for younger children, especially having children role play positive solutions to conflict situations that are presented to them in the classroom setting.

Older children and adolescents may not only rely more on scenarios that require them to answer a series of questions concerning positive and negative responses to conflict, attitudes, and feelings of children who are confronted with a potential peer sexual harassment, but also strategies for reporting their experiences to teachers, parents, and school administrators. Films, videos, and role playing can also, of course, be valuable resources for this age group.

Establishing an Atmosphere of Trust. In addition to taking into consideration the children's level of cognitive maturity, those designing curriculum projects must make it a priority to accomplish the goals of the training without creating undue anxiety for children and adolescents. Trainers must be able to relate well to a variety of children, so that the children will feel comfortable talking with them and listening to them about the legal and psychological issues involved. Trainers must also be able to discuss sexuality and deviant behavior without blushing, passing judgment, or exhibiting signs of disapproval. Trainers must establish rapport and a respectful atmosphere in training sessions in which children's and adolescents' feelings of anger, confusion, fear, and mistrust can be expressed without fear of being ridiculed or retaliated against. This is especially crucial in answering questions regarding sexuality, physical development accompanying puberty, and sexual orientation—all areas of concern for adolescents.

Ensuring Support Outside the Classroom. Inviting parents, members of the school board, and other concerned individuals to participate in the curriculum projects can ensure support outside the classroom. Several organizations may be contacted for participation in the programs, even to the extent of teaching a module in an area pertinent to their expertise. Examples of such organizations include: American Association of University Women, YWCA, YMCA, Girl Scouts, Boys and Girls Clubs. Trainers should work with any interested parents on ways to reinforce the messages of the curriculum project at home.

Training Factors to Consider. Consideration must be given to the following questions prior to the initiation of any training program:

- What provisions does the school have for children and adolescents who wish to report an experience that was prompted by the training?
- Does the school have trained child and/or school psychologists available during and following the training session to assist with children or adolescents who have flashbacks or are visibly upset?
- Did the school obtain parental permission for the training program?
- What follow-up to the training programs have been put in place?
- How often will the training programs be offered?
- What means of reinforcing the information from the training program will be instituted?

Additional Responsibilities of Schools. In addition to the enforcement of a policy, investigatory procedures, and training programs for children and adolescents, school districts may want to consider the following programs to meet their mission of providing education on sexual harassment:

- Information-based seminars for school personnel concerning sexual harassment
- Information-based presentations for parents concerning the school's active role in preventing sexual harassment

- Development of brochures, pamphlets, and posters describing the school's efforts in policies, procedures, and training
- Information-based Student Sexual Harassment Awareness Week
- Encouragement of teachers to incorporate discussions of sexual harassment in their courses.

SEXUAL HARASSMENT: A FORM OF SEXISM
IN ELEMENTARY AND SECONDARY SCHOOLS

Sexism refers to the unjustified selectively negative behavior against women or men as members of a social category. It is particularly used to denote discrimination against girls and women. Research has suggested four levels of sexism: individual, social/structural, institutional, and cultural that interact with each other. Part of the definition of gender roles in Western culture involves assumptions about the types of occupations, life-styles, and abilities that are held to be appropriate for girls and boys. Distinctions have been in agreement with traditional stereotypes about personality traits. For example, boys and men typically have been described by a series of characteristics that reflect rationality, assertiveness, and competency (i.e., objectivity, self-confidence, independence). Occupations stereotyped by individuals as "male-appropriate" that are associated with these personality characteristics include attorney, police officer, physician, and corporate officer. Traits such as submissive, subjective, emotional, caring, and gentle have been used to describe girls and women. Traditional "female-appropriate" occupations include elementary school teacher, typist, librarian, and nurse. Both masculine personality characteristics and occupations are generally rated by women and men as more desirable, important, and prestigious.

Sexist attitudes may lead to sexist behavior or sex discrimination against girls. For example, Nancy Betz (1993) has argued that the early schooling children receive is not only a major source of gender role socialization, but also a source of messages concerning appropriate behaviors and rules for girls and boys, women, and men. Research by Myra Sadker and David Sadker (1994) suggests that teachers give boys more attention than girls. Boys are more likely to receive positive feedback, more likely to be recognized for their creativity, more likely to be called on in class, and more likely to be included in verbal interactions.

In another study, teachers were asked to name the students whom they often thought about after school hours (Ben-Tsvi-Mayer, Hertz-Lazarowitz, and Safir 1989). Results suggested that teachers were 61 percent more likely to list boys than to list girls. Thus, research on the treatment of girls in elementary and secondary school suggested a pattern of invisibility. Sadker and Sadker argued that such "sexism in our schools is crippling tomorrow's women."

Teachers' behavior can be influential. Attempts at encouraging change in teachers' behavior (and attitudes) must be part of any training program. We recommend faculty development seminars for alerting teachers to their possible differential treatment of girls and boys and to the hostile environment for girls in the classroom created by such treatment.

We also recommend that school administrators monitor both the tests and the textbooks that are given to school children, since intelligence and achievement tests as well as children's readers are frequently stereotyped.

An African proverb says it takes a whole village to educate a child: in our schools this means parents, grandparents, teachers, school administrators, and legislators. As Sadker and Sadker (1994) state:

> When all these citizens from our American village join forces, they can transform our educational institutions into the most powerful levers for equity, places where girls are valued as much as boys, daughters cherished as fully as sons, and tomorrow's women are prepared to be full partners in all activities of the next century and beyond. (p. 280)

RESOURCES
FOR EDUCATING
CHILDREN AND ADOLESCENTS
ABOUT SEXUAL HARASSMENT

Sample Curricula for Elementary School Students

TOTAL TIME FOR TRAINING PROGRAM: 3 CLASS PERIODS

Overall Goals of Training Program

- Define quid pro quo and hostile environment sexual harassment.
- Discuss the physical and emotional reactions to being sexually harassed.
- Discuss peer sexual harassment.
- Discuss means of resolution for complaints of sexual harassment.

Overall Objectives of Training Program

At the conclusion of this training program, students will be able to:

1. Assess their own perceptions of sexual harassment.
2. Label adequately behaviors as illustrative of sexual harassment or not illustrative of sexual harassment.
3. Identify peer sexual harassment.
4. Describe the effects of sexual harassment on students.
5. State the proper procedure to follow if sexual harassment occurs.

Topics for Presentation and Discussion

Lesson 1   Introduction to Program and Definition of Sexual Harassment
(1 class period)

Objectives

At the conclusion of this class, students will be able to:

- Assess their own perceptions of sexual harassment.
- Label adequately behaviors as illustrative of sexual harassment or not illustrative of sexual harassment.
- Identify peer sexual harassment.

- State the difference between flirting and sexual harassment.

Introduction

- Trainer welcomes students to the class.
- Trainer introduces her/himself to students.
- Students introduce themselves and offer goals for training.
- Trainer writes these responses on the flipchart/chalkboard for all students to see.
- Trainer summarizes students' responses.
- Trainer states goals for training session.

Definition of Sexual Harassment

- Trainer reads sexual harassment case studies and/or does role playing.
- Students answer trainer-directed questions.
- Trainer lectures and leads guided discussion of sexual harassment.
- Trainer makes summary comments from this unit.
- Trainer summarizes major points from lesson.
- Trainer identifies goals of next class period.

Lesson 2   What are the Causes and the Impact of Sexual Harassment?
(1 class period)

Objectives

At the conclusion of this class, students will be able to:

- Assess their perceptions of the effects of sexual harassment on students.
- Identify emotional, physical, and career development effects of sexual harassment.
- Assess contributing factors to sexual harassment.

Presentation

- Trainer reviews major points from first class period.
- Trainer lectures on the impact of sexual harassment on students.

- Trainer dramatizes a case study, and/or role playing.
- Trainer leads guided discussion with case studies.
- Trainer makes summary comments from this unit.
- Trainer identifies goals of next class period.

Lesson 3   Stopping Sexual Harassment
     (1 class period)

Objectives

At the conclusion of this class, students will be able to:

- Determine action to take if a student experiences sexual harassment.
- Determine solutions to incidents of sexual harassment.
- Examine the school's policy on sexual harassment.
- Identify educational programs to help their school deal with sexual harassment.
- Summarize major issues in sexual harassment identified in three class periods.

Presentation

- Trainer reviews information from previous two classes by using flipchart/chalkboard.
- Trainer announces goals of final class period devoted to sexual harassment.
- Trainer asks students to list ways they can work with their school in preventing sexual harassment.
- Trainer posts these responses on the flipchart/ chalkboard.
- Trainer distributes copies of school's policy statement on sexual harassment for students' parents.
- Trainer introduces individual charged with implementing policy statement. (Optional)
- Trainer asks students to list additional educational programs for their school.

- Trainer works with students in preparing material on sexual harassment for a classroom bulletin board.
- Trainer reviews major points from three class periods.
- Trainer rereads case studies to students and answers questions.
- Trainer meets individually with students who wish to speak to her/him privately.

Sample Curricula for Secondary School Students

TOTAL TIME FOR TRAINING PROGRAM: 3 CLASS PERIODS

Overall Goals of Training Program

- Define quid pro quo and hostile environment sexual harassment.
- Discuss the physical and emotional reactions to being sexually harassed.
- Discuss peer sexual harassment.
- Discuss means of resolving complaints of sexual harassment.

Overall Objectives of Training Program

At the conclusion of this training program, students will be able to:

- Assess their own perceptions of sexual harassment.
- Label adequately behaviors as illustrative of sexual harassment, or not illustrative of sexual harassment.
- Identify peer sexual harassment.
- Describe the effects of sexual harassment on students.
- State the proper procedure to follow if sexual harassment occurs.

Topics for Presentation and Discussion

Lesson 1 Introduction to Program and Definition of Sexual Harassment
(1 class period)

Objectives

At the conclusion of this class, students will be able to:

- Assess their own perceptions of sexual harassment.
- Label adequately behaviors as illustrative of sexual harassment, or not illustrative of sexual harassment.
- Identify peer sexual harassment.
- State the difference between flirting and sexual harassment.

Introduction

- Trainer welcomes students to the class.
- Trainer introduces her/him self to students.
- Students introduce themselves and state one question they want to have answered in the training sessions.
- Trainer writes these answers on the flipchart/chalkboard for all students to see.
- Trainer summarizes students' responses.
- Trainer states goals for training session.

Definition of Sexual Harassment

- Trainer distributes copies of sexual harassment case study.
- In small groups, students read case study to answer trainer-directed questions.
- Trainer lectures and leads guided discussion of sexual harassment.
- Trainer makes summary comments from this unit.

Lesson 2   What are the Causes and the Impact of Sexual Harassment?
(1 class period)

Objectives

At the conclusion of this class, students will be able to:

- Assess their perceptions of the effects of sexual harassment on students.
- Identify emotional, physical, and career development effects of sexual harassment.
- Assess contributing factors to sexual harassment.

Presentation

- Trainer reviews major points from first class period.
- Trainer discusses the boundaries of gender and power.
- Trainer lectures on the impact of sexual harassment on students.
- Trainer makes summary comments from this unit.
- Trainer identifies goals of next class period.

Lesson 3   Stopping Sexual Harassment
(1 class period)

Objectives

At the conclusion of this class, students will be able to:

1. Determine action to take if a student experiences sexual harassment.
2. Determine solutions to incidents of sexual harassment.
3. Examine the school's policy on sexual harassment.
4. Identify educational programs to help their school deal with sexual harassment.
5. Summarize major issues in sexual harassment identified in three class periods.

Presentation

- Trainer reviews information from previous two classes by using flipchart/chalkboard.
- Trainer announces goals of final class period devoted to sexual harassment.
- Trainer asks students to list ways they can work with their school in preventing sexual harassment.
- Trainer posts these responses on the flipchart/chalkboard.
- Trainer distributes copies of school's policy statement on sexual harassment.
- Trainer introduces individual charged with implementing policy statement. (Optional)
- Trainer leads guided discussion of policy statement.
- Trainer asks students to list additional educational programs for their school.
- Trainer reviews major points from three class periods.
- Trainer asks students to reread case study and answer questions.
- Trainer works with students in preparing bulletin boards on issues related to sexual harassment.
- Trainer meets individually with students who wish to speak to her/him privately.

Sample Case Studies for
Elementary and Secondary School Students

FOR ELEMENTARY SCHOOL STUDENTS

Jamie is in the _____ grade—just like all of you. One day on the playground at school, two of the boys in her class, Billy and Carlos, stood on either side of Jamie. Billy and Carlos grabbed Jamie's pants and pulled them down to her ankles. All the children on the playground looked at Jamie.

Questions to Consider when Reading and Discussing Case Studies with Elementary School Students

Questions to Be Read to Children for Discussion:

• How do you think Jamie felt when Billy and Carlos pulled her pants down around her ankles?
• Do you think Jamie felt like crying?
• Do you think any of the children laughed? Why?
• Do you think Billy and Carlos should have pulled Jamie's pants down?
• How do you think Jamie felt when she had to go into school after playing outside?
• Do you think Jamie should tell her teacher what Billy and Carlos did to her?
• What do you think Jamie's teacher should do?
• What should happen to Billy and Carlos?
• What would you say to Jamie if you knew her?
• What would you say to Billy and Carlos if you knew them?

Jennifer and Patrick are friends. One day Patrick tells Jennifer that he saw some graffiti written about her in the boys' bathroom. The graffiti was about how Jennifer probably looks without her clothes on. After Patrick told Jennifer about the boys' bathroom, Jennifer started to notice boys in her class laughing at her. Jennifer has been staying home from school.

Questions to Consider when Reading and Discussing Case Studies with Elementary School Students

Questions to Be Read to Children for Discussion:

• How do you think Jennifer feels?
• Why do you think she has been staying home from school?
• Do you think Jennifer feels like crying? Why?
• Why do you think Patrick told Jennifer?
• Why are the boys in Jennifer's class laughing at her?

- Do you think Jennifer's teacher should saying something to the boys? What should she say?
- How would you feel if you were Jennifer?
- How would you feel if you were Patrick?
- What should happen to the boys who wrote the graffiti about Jennifer?
- What would you say to Jennifer if you knew her?

For Secondary School Students

In her math class, Yolanda's teacher smiles and comments on her appearance as a greeting each morning. Yolanda notices that no other student in the class gets this treatment—just her. Yolanda knows she is not being complimented by her teacher. One day, Yolanda's teacher asked her to wear sweaters more often—that she looks "real good" in them because of the size of her breasts.On another day, Yolanda's teacher told her to sit in the front of the room. Yolanda remembers that the only time she is asked to sit in the front of the room is when she is wearing a skirt or dress, never when she is wearing pants. And, last week, one day before class started, Yolanda's teacher tells the whole math class that Yolanda should be a model for "men's magazines" because of the way she has developed.

Questions to Consider when Reading and Discussing Case Study with Secondary School Students

- How do you think Yolanda feels? Is she scared? upset? angry? embarassed? guilty?
- Does the behavior outlined in this case study seem inappropriate to you? Why or why not?
- Do you believe the behavior described in the case study illustrates sexual harassment? Why or why not?
- If yes, what kind of sexual harassment do you believe this case study illustrates? quid pro quo or hostile environment sexual harassment?

- What do you think Yolanda should do?
- What do you think Yolanda's teacher should do?
- What do you think Yolanda's classmates think about her?
- What do you think Yolanda's classmates think about their math teacher?
- Pretend you are in this math class with Yolanda. What, if anything, would you say to her? Why?
- Pretend you are in this math class with Yolanda. What, if anything, would you say to the teacher? Why? What, if anything, would you do? Why?
- What services would be available at your school to assist with the situations described?
- If you were the student in this case study, what services would you want, if any, to assist you?
- Do you belive the sex or sexual orientation of the individuals in the case study make any difference in your evaluation of the situation?
- What outcome would you like to see in this case? Explain.
- Is discussing the case difficult? Why or why not?

The girls have to walk in front of the boys in the gymnasium so they can get to their side of the gym for their class. Many boys hang out along the side of the gym where the girls have to walk and make comments and noises about the girls' appearance as they pass. They rate the girls on a scale of 1 to 10.

Questions to Consider when Reading and Discussing Case Study with Secondary School Students

- Do you think this is sexual harassment? Why or why not?
- How do you think the girls feel?
- What do you think the boys should do?
- What do you think the girls' gym teacher should do?
- What do you think the boys' gym teacher should do?

- Pretend you are in this gym class. How would you feel if the boys rated your body?
- What services would be available at your school to assist with the situations described?
- If you were a girl student in this case study, what services would you want, if any, to assist you?
- What outcome would you like to see in this case? Explain.

Educational Techniques for Discussing Sexual Harassment with Students

- Ask students to list behaviors they believe illustrate "flirting." Then ask students to indicate how they feel when they are flirting, and when they are the recipients of flirtatious behavior. Ask students to list examples of behavior that is sexual harassment. Then ask students how they feel when they have been sexually harassed. Have students distinguish between flirting and sexual harassment.
- Ask students to design a play that deals with the sexual harassment of a high school student by another student. Have students list the issues they believe should be acted out in the play. Put on the play for parents. Distribute copies of the school's policy statement to parents and facilitate a general discussion about what the school is doing to establish and maintain a sexual harassment-free environment.
- Host a Sexual Harassment Awareness Week at your school. During this week, invite speakers to give presentations about various aspects of sexual harassment to students, employees, and teachers. Show films and present student-led discussions.
- Hold a poster contest that deals with the theme, Sexual Harassment is No Joke.
- Invite students to help write a public service announcement about sexual harassment that can be broadcast throughout the school.

- Ask students to collect newspaper and magazine articles about sexual harassment and bring them to their class. Display these articles on the class bulletin board.
- Invite students to help design a school bulletin board that deals with sexual harassment prevention.
- Invite parents to cofacilitate training programs on sexual harassment awareness.
- Use small group discussions in class, focused on sample scenarios, to explore students' reactions to issues of sexual harassment.

Checklist for School Administrators

- Monitor the posting of the school's policy statement and investigatory procedures.
- Monitor the publication of the policy statement and investigatory procedures in teacher/staff handbooks.
- Check bathroom walls daily for inappropriate graffiti. Wash and/or paint the walls when needed.
- Include the sexual harassment policy in the student handbook, taking into account age-appropriate language.
- Award students and teachers who serve as positive role models by their treatment of individuals with respect and dignity.
- Establish a peer mentoring program for older students to teach younger ones about sexual harassment.
- Use sex-inclusive language in all classes and activities.
- Facilitate seminars for teachers on avoiding sex discrimination and gender stereotyping in the classroom.
- Train all staff in sexual harassment awareness and prevention.

- Establish a School Climate Committee whose task it is to monitor the incidence of sexual harassment at the school.

Faculty Development Seminars
on Gender Equity in the Classroom

SEMINAR 1

Lecture/Presentation:Sexism
Teachers' Role in Fostering Gender Equity in the Classroom
Small Group Discussion about Teachers' Pedagogical Techniques

Readings:

American Association of University Women. 1993. *Hostile Hallways: The AAUW Survey on Sexual Harassment in America's Schools.* Washington, DC: Author.

Sadker, M., and D. Sadker. 1994. *Failing at Fairness: How America's Schools Cheat Girls.* New York: Scribner.

SEMINAR 2

Lecture/Presentation: Gender Equity in Texts and Readers
Small Group Discussion of Alternative Readings that Promote Gender Equity

Readings:

Kay, M. 1975. "The Role of Male and Female in Children's Picture Books—Dispelling All Doubt." In *Woman: Dependent or Independent Variable.* Edited by R. Unger & F. Denmark. New York: Psychological Dimensions.

Borderlon, K. W. 1985. "Sexism in Reading Materials." *Reading Teacher* 38: 792–797.

Excerpts from Sadker and Sadker. 1994.

SEMINAR 3

Lecture/Presentation:Communicating Verbally and Nonverbally
Discussion of Alternative Communication Patterns

Readings:

Lakoff, R. 1975. *Language and Women's Place*. New York: Harper and Row.

Lipton, J., and A. Hershaft. 1984. "Girl," "Woman," "Guy," "Man": The Effects of Sexist Labelling. *Sex Roles* 10: 183–194.

Tannen, D. 1990. *You Just Don't Understand: Women and Men in Conversations*. New York: Morrow.

SEMINAR 4

- Discussion of individual issues with gender-equity in the classroom.
- Faculty reports on ways to gender-balance in the curriculum.
- Suggestions for follow-up to faculty development seminars.

Suggestions for Teachers for Establishing Gender-Equity in the Classroom

1. When making general statements about girls (or any other group), be sure that they are based on accurate information. Universal generalizations about any social group, such as, "Girls don't think

geographically," are likely, at best, to represent uncritical oversimplifications of selected norms.

2. Avoid humorous or gratuitous remarks that demean or belittle people because of sex, sexual orientation, race, religion, or physical characteristics. Respect the dignity of all students.

3. Avoid using generic masculine terms to refer to people of both sexes. Although the effort to do this may involve some initial discomfort, it will result in more precise communication and understanding.

4. When using illustrative examples, avoid stereotypes, such as making all authority figures boys and all subordinates girls.

5. Try to monitor your behavior toward students in the classroom. (You might ask a friend to observe your classes.) Ask, for example:
   - Do you give more time to boys than to girls?
   - Do you give more time to nonminority than to minority students?
   - Do you treat boys more seriously than girls? nonminority students more seriously than minority students?
   - Are you systematically more attentive to questions, observations, and responses made by students of one sex or race? or age?
   - Do you direct more of your own questions, observations, and responses to students of one sex or race or age?
   - Do you assume a heterosexual model when referring to human behavior?

6. Choose course material which does not perpetuate sexual and racial stereotypes.

Components of an Effective Policy Statement for Elementary and Secondary Schools

- Write a philosophy statement that sexual harassment is illegal and won't be tolerated.

- Definition of sexual harassment, including peer sexual harassment.
- Give examples of behaviors that constitute sexual harassment.
- Issue a statement outlining the impact of sexual harassment on students.
- Encourage students' responsibility to report sexual harassment.
- Outline the school's responsibility in responding to a report of sexual harassment.
- Make a statement concerning confidentiality.
- Explain the investigatory process.
- Issue a statement concerning sanctions for sexual harassment, sanctions for retaliation, and false complaints.
- Give an identification of individual(s) responsible for hearing complaints, and the personnel and services available (e.g, nurses, guidance counselors).

SOME SUGGESTIONS

1. Draft the policy statement in sex neutral terms; the statement will enhance the acceptance of sexual harassment-free environments by all individuals.
2. The policy statement should contain an alternative procedure for complaints if the investigator is the alleged harasser.
3. Claims of sexual harassment should not be trivialized but treated seriously. All claims must be thoroughly investigated before any action is taken. Should an individual feel that she/he is in physical danger, changes must be made in the classroom. Suggestions concerning notifying police must also be provided.
4. The policy statement must be available in foreign languages in addition to English.

5. The policy statement must be revised when new case law and state law modifications deem it appropriate.
6. The policy statement must be reissued every year and sent to all members of the school community as well as posted throughout the school and in handbooks.

Discussing Sexual Harassment in Secondary School Classes

MATHEMATICS

- Methodology used to obtain incidence rates of sexual harassment.
- Scaling of scenarios depicting sexual harassment for severity.
- Survey construction.

SOCIAL STUDIES

- Interface of gender, race, and power involved in sexual harassment.
- Social policy applications of research on sexual harassment.
- Attitudes toward victim blame and victim responsibility.

HOME ECONOMICS/CHILD DEVELOPMENT

- Incidence of sexual harassment among children and adolescents.
- Socialization agents contributing to acceptance of sexual harassment.
- Symptoms associated with Sexual Harassment Trauma Syndrome.

FOR GUIDANCE COUNSELORS

- Sexual harassment as a barrier to career development.

PSYCHOLOGY/SOCIOLOGY

- Relationship between sexual harassment and incest, battering, and rape.
- Manifestations of power abuses in educational and work settings.

REFERENCES

American Association of University Women. 1993. *Hostile Hallways*. Washington, DC: Author.

Ben Tsvi-Mayer, S., R. Hertz-Lazarowitz, and M. Safir. 1980. "Teachers' Selections of Boys and Girls as Prominent Pupils. *Sex Roles* 21: 231–245.

Betz, N. 1993. "Women's Career Development." In *Psychology of Women: A Handbook of Issues and Theories*. Edited by F. Denmark and M. A. Paludi. Westport, CT: Greenwood Press.

Bogart, K., S. Simmons, N. Stein, and E. Tomaszewski. 1992. "Breaking the Silence: Sexual and Gender-Based Harassment in Elementary, Secondary, and Postsecondary Education." In *Sex Equity and Sexuality in Education*. Edited by S. Klein. Albany: State University of New York Press.

Brooks, L., and A. Perot. 1991. "Reporting Sexual Harassment: Exploring a Predictive Model." *Psychology of Women Quarterly* 15: 31–47.

Chamberlain, E. October 1994. "Power, Consent, and Adolescent Sexual Harassment." Paper presented at the Meeting of the Northeastern Educational Research Association, Ellenville, NY.

Corbett, K. 1993. "Sexual Harassment in High School." *Youth and Society* 25: 93–103.

Doyle, J., and M. A. Paludi. 1995. *Sex and Gender: The Human Experience*. Dubuque, IA: William C. Brown.

Fitzgerald, L., and A. Omerod. 1993. "Sexual Harassment in Academia and the Workplace." In *Psychology of Women:*

A Handbook of Issues and Theories. Edited by F. Denmark and M. A. Paludi. Westport, CT: Greenwood Press.

Malovich, N., and J. Stake. 1990. "Sexual Harassment on Campus. *Psychology of Women Quarterly* 14: 63–81.

Paludi, M. A. November 1993. "Ivory Power Revisited: Changed Individuals, Changed Campuses." Paper presented at the Vermont Women in Higher Education Conference, Burlington, VT.

———. 1996. *Sexual Harassment on College Campuses: Abusing the Ivory Power.* Albany: State University of New York Press.

Phinney, G. S. 1994. "Sexual Harassment: A Dynamic Element in the Lives of Middle School Girls and Teachers." *Equity and Excellence in Education* 27: 5–10.

Roscoe, B. 1994. "Sexual Harassment: An Educational Program for Middle School Students." *Elementary School Guidance and Counseling* 29: 110–120.

———. 1994. "Sexual Harassment: Early Adolescents' Self-reports of Experiences and Acceptance." *Adolescence* 29: 515–523.

Sadker, M., and D. Sadker. 1994. *Failing at Fairness.* New York: Scribners.

Sandler, B., and M. A. Paludi. 1992. *Educator's Guide to Controlling Sexual Harassment.* Washington, DC: Thompson.

Stein, N. 1993. "Secrets in Public: Sexual Harassment in Public and Private Schools." Working Paper, Wellesley College, No. 256.

———. April 1994. "Seeing Is Not Believing: Sexual Harassment in Public School and the Role of Adults." Paper presented at the Annual Meeting of the American Educational Research Association, New Orleans, LA.

Turner, P. 1995. "Sensitivity to Verbally and Physically Harassing Behaviors and Reported Incidents in Junior High/Middle School Students." Master's thesis, Fort Hays State University.

APPENDIX I

Additional Resources for Trainers,
Counselors, and Administrators

Audio-Visual Material

YOUR RIGHT TO FIGHT:
STOPPING SEXUAL HARASSMENT ON CAMPUS
Affirmative Action AD 301
State University of New York at Albany
Albany, NY 12222

THE WRONG IDEA
Minnesota Women's Center
5 Eddy Hall
192 Pillsbury Drive SE
University of Minnesota
Minneapolis, MN 55455

SEXUAL HARASSMENT ON CAMPUS:
CURRENT CONCERNS AND CONSIDERATIONS
Center for Instructional Services
Old Dominion University
Norfolk, VA 23529

YOU ARE THE GAME: SEXUAL HARASSMENT
Indiana University
Audio Visual Center
Bloomington, IN 47405

INTENT VS. IMPACT
BNA Communications Inc.
9439 Key West Avenue
Rockville, MD 20850

SEX, POWER, AND THE WORKPLACE
KCET Video
4401 Sunset Blvd.
Los Angeles, CA 90027

NO LAUGHING MATTER:
HIGH SCHOOL STUDENTS AND SEXUAL HARASSMENT
Massachusetts Department of Education
1385 Hancock Street
Quincy, MA 02169

SEXUAL HARASSMENT:
BUILDING AWARENESS ON CAMPUS
The Media Education Foundation
26 Center St.
Northampton, MA 01060

TEEN AWARENESS: SEXUAL HARASSMENT—
WHAT IT IS, WHAT TO DO
New Dimension Media
85803 Lorane Highway
Eugene, OR 97405

MEN AND WOMEN PARTNERS AT WORK
Dynamics of Human Behavior
1693 Alameda de la Pulgas
Redwood City, CA 94061

WORKPLACE HUSTLE
Aims Media Inc.
9710 DeSoto Ave.
Chatworth, CA 91311

SEXUAL HARASSMENT CROSSING THE LINE
Cambridge Career Products
P.O. Box 2153 Department CC13
Charleston, WV 25328

SEXUAL ABUSE AND HARASSMENT CAUSES, PREVENTION, AND COPING
Guidance Associates
90 South Bedford Rd.
Mt. Kisko, NY 10549

SEXUAL HARASSMENT IN THE SCHOOLS
Northwest Women's Law Center
119 South Main St. Suite 330
Seattle, WA 98104

SEXUAL HARASSMENT: ISSUES AND ANSWERS
College and University Personnel Association
1233 20th St. NW
Washington, DC 20036

WOULD YOU LET SOMEONE DO THIS TO YOUR SISTER?
Women's Rights Department
United Auto Workers
8000 East Jefferson Ave.
Detroit, MI 48214

For additional information regarding audio-visual material, the following may be contacted:

Cambridge Documentary Films
P.O. Box 385
Cambridge, MA 02139
(617) 354-3677

Dancing Can Productions
Box 5540
Berkeley, CA 94705
(510) 547-7544

Disabled Women's Theatre Project
462 Broadway
New York, NY 10013
(212) 925-0606

Iris Films
Box 5353
Berkeley, CA 94705
(510) 845-5414

Ishtar Films
6253 Hollywood Blvd.
Hollywood, CA 90028
(213) 461-1560

Moonforce Media
P.O. Box 2934
Washington, DC 20013
(301) 585-8886

Newist
IS110 University of Wisconsin
Green Bay, WI 54311
(414) 465-2576

Wolfe Video
P.O. Box 64
New Alamaden, CA 95042
(408) 268-6782

Women Make Movies
462 Broadway
New York, NY 10013
(212) 925-0606

Organizations

For additional information regarding 1-800 numbers, contact the Toll Free Directory published by AT&T. We also recommend consulting the following directory of organizations in the United States: *Encyclopedia of Associations*. It is published by Gale Research Inc. 835 Penobscot Bldg. Detroit, MI 48226. A recommended directory of women's organizations entitled *The Women's Information Exchange National Directory* is compiled by Deborah Brecher and Jill Lippitt and is published by Avon Books.

Women in Crisis: 1–800–992–1101
**Rape and Victim Assistance
Center:** 1–800–422–3204

ORGANIZATIONS

Women Against Pornography
358 W. 47th St.
New York, NY 10036

9 to 5
YWCA
140 Clarendon St.
Boston, MA 02139

Equal Employment Opportunity Commission
2401 E Street NW
Washington, DC 20506

National Organization for Victim Assistance
1757 Park Rd. NW
Washington, DC 20010

National Woman Abuse Prevention Project
1112 16th St. NW
Washington, DC 20036

Center for Women's Policy Studies
2000 P Street, NW
Suite 508
Washington, DC 20036

Coalition of Labor Union Women
15 Union Square
New York, NY 10003

Equal Rights Advocates
1663 Mission Street
Suite 550
San Francisco, CA 94103

Federally Employed Women
1400 I Street, NW
Washington, DC 20005

Fund for the Feminist Majority
1600 Wison Boulevard
Suite 704
Arlington, VA 22209

NOW Legal Defense and Education Fund
99 Hudson Street
New York, NY 10013

National Network of Minority Women in Science
Association for the Advancement of Science
1776 Massachusetts Ave. NW
Washington, DC 20036

Pacific Resource Development Group
4044 NE 58th Street
Seattle, WA 98105

Wider Opportunities for Women
1325 G Street, NW
Washington, DC 20005

Women Employed
22 West Monroe
Suite 1400
Chicago, IL 60603

Women's Legal Defense Fund
1875 Connecticut Avenue, NW
Washington, DC 20009

National University Continuing Education Association
Division of Women's Education
One Dupont Circle
Washington, DC 20036

American Educational Research Association
1230 17 St. NW
Washington, DC 20036

Sexual Harassment Coalitions/Organizations

Canadian Association
Against Sexual Harassment
Dr. Carole Pond
Sexual Harassment Office
University of Saskatchewan
104 Qu'Appelle Hall Addition
Saskatoon, Saskatchewan, Canada S7N 0W0

Sociologists Against Sexual Harassment
Dr. James Gruber
Sociology Department
University of Michigan
Dearborn, MI 48128

Women's Political Groups

Alabama Women's Agenda
3414 7th St. S
Birmingham, AL 35222
(205) 324-6947

American Political Science Association
Committee on the Status of Women
    in Political Science
1527 New Hampshire Ave. NW
Washington, DC 20036
(202) 483-2512

Arkansas Women's Political Caucus
P.O. Box 2494
Little Rock, AR 72203
(501) 376-7913

Capital Hill Women's Political Caucus
Longworth House Office Bldg.
P.O. Box 599
Washington, DC 20515
(202) 986-0994

Center for the American Woman and Politics
Eagleton Institute of Politics
Rutgers University
New Brunswick, NJ 08901
(908) 828-2210

Coalition for Women's Appointments
National Women's Political Caucus
1275 K St. NW
Washington, DC 20005
(202) 898-1100

Fifty/Fifty by 2000
P.O. Box 34
Fairfield, CT 06430
(203) 259-1446

**International Institute for Women's
Political Leadership**
1511 K St. NW
Washington, DC 20005
(202) 842-1523

League of Women Voters
1730 M St. NW
Washington, DC 20036
(202) 429-1965

Massachusetts Women's Political Caucus
145 Tremont St.
Boston, MA 02111
(617) 451-9294

National Association of Commissions for Women
2000 14th St. NW
Washington, DC 20009
(202) 628-5030

National Order of Women Legislators
1300 Berkeley Rd.
Columbia, SC 29205
(803) 734-0480

National Women's Party
144 Constitution Ave. NE
Washington, DC 20002
(202) 546-1210

Women Organizing Women
P.O. Box 1652
New Haven, CT 06507
(203) 281-3400

Women's Action Coalition
P.O. Box 131148
Houston, TX 77219
(713) 867-9581

Women's Vote Project
1601 Connecticut Ave. NW
Washington, DC 20009
(202) 328-2312

Resource Guides and Reports
on Sexual Harassment

**FLIRTING OR HURTING? A TEACHER'S GUIDE ON
STUDENT-TO-STUDENT SEXUAL HARASSMENT IN SCHOOLS**
Wellesley College Center for Research on Women
106 Central Street
Wellesley, MA 02181

**SEXUAL HARASSMENT AND TEENS:
A PROGRAM FOR POSITIVE CHANGE**
Free Spirit Publishing, Inc.
400 First Avenue North Suite 515
Minneapolis, MN 55401

**TUNE-IN TO YOUR RIGHTS: A GUIDE FOR TEENAGERS
ABOUT TURNING OFF SEXUAL HARASSMENT**
Programs for Educational Opportunity
1005 School of Education
University of Michigan
Ann Arbor, MI 48109

STOPPING SEXUAL HARASSMENT
Labor Education and Research Project
7435 Michigan Avenue
Detroit, MI 48210

9 TO 5 GUIDE TO COMBATTING SEXUAL HARASSMENT
National Association of Working Women
614 Superior Avenue NW
Cleveland, OH 44113

**SEXUAL HARASSMENT AND EMPLOYMENT DISCRIMINATION
AGAINST WOMEN: A CONSUMER HANDBOOK FOR
WOMEN WHO ARE HARMED, AND FOR THOSE WHO CARE**
Feminist Institute Clearinghouse
PO Box 30563
Bethesda, MD 20824

SEXUAL HARASSMENT: RESEARCH AND RESOURCES
National Council for Research on Women
530 Broadway at Spring St. 10th Floor
New York, NY 10012

SEXUAL HARASSMENT: BUILDING A CONSENSUS FOR CHANGE
Report by Governor Cuomo's Task Force
on Sexual Harassment
Division for Women
2 World Trade Center
Executive Chamber
New York, NY 10047

Related Readings

WORKPLACE SEXUAL HARASSMENT

Baker, N. 1989. "Sexual Harassment and Job Satisfaction in Traditional and Nontraditional Industrial Occupations." Ph.D. diss. California School of Professional Psychology, Los Angeles.

Blaxall, M., B. Parsonson, and N. Robertson. 1993. "The Development and Evaluation of a Sexual Harassment Contact Person Training Package." *Behavior Modification* 17: 148–163.

Connell, D. 1991. "Effective Sexual Harassment Policies: Unexpected Lessons from Jacksonville Shipyards." *Employee Relations* 17: 191–206.

Crull, P. 1982. "Stress Effects of Sexual Harassment on the Job: Implications for Counseling." *American Journal of Orthopsychiatry* 52: 539–544.

Duhon, D. 1993. "Sexual Harassment in the Workplace: A Review of the Legal Rights and Responsibilities of All Parties." *Public Personnel Management* 22: 123–135.

Ehrenreich, N. 1990. "Pluralist Myths and Powerless Men: The Ideology of Reasonableness in Sexual Harassment Law. *Yale Law Review* 99: 1207–1208.

Fitzgerald, L. F. 1993. "Sexual Harassment: Violence Against Women in the Workplace. *American Psychologist* 48: 1070–1076.

Fitzgerald, L. F., and A. Ormerod. 1993. "Sexual Harassment in Academia and the Workplace. In *Psychology of Women: A Handbook of Issues and Theories*. Edited by F. Denmark and M. A. Paludi. Westport, CT: Greenwood Press.

Fitzgerald, L. F., S. Shullman, N. Bailey, M. Richards, J. Swecker, A. Gold, A. Ormerod, and L. Weitzman. 1988. "The Incidence and Dimensions of Sexual Harassment in Academia and the Workplace. *Journal of Vocational Behavior* 32: 152–175.

Gold, Y. August 1987. "The Sexualization of the Workplace: Sexual Harassment of Pink-, White- and Blue-Collar Workers." Paper presented to the annual conference of the American Psychological Association, New York.

Gutek, B. 1985. *Sex and the Workplace*. San Francisco: Jossey-Bass.

———. 1993. "Sexual Harassment Rights and Responsibilities." *Employee Responsibilities and Rights Journal* 6: 325–340.

Gutek, B., and M. Koss. 1993. "Changed Women and Changed Organizations: Consequences of and Coping with Sexual Harassment." *Journal of Vocational Behavior* 42: 28–48.

Hames, D. 1994. "Disciplining Sexual Harassers: What's Fair?" *Employee Responsibilities and Rights Journal* 7: 207–217.

LaFontaine, E., and L. Tredeau. 1986. "The Frequency, Sources, and Correlates of Sexual Harassment Among Women in Traditional Male Occupations." *Sex Roles* 15: 423–432.

Levy, A., and M. A. Paludi. 1997. *Workplace Sexual Harassment.* Englewood Cliffs, NJ: Prentice Hall.

Morris, C. 1994. *Bearing Witness: Sexual Harassment and Beyond—Everywoman's Story.* Boston: Little, Brown.

Newell, C., P. Rosenfeld, and A. Culbertson. 1995. "Sexual Harassment Experiences and Equal Opportunity Perceptions of Navy Women." *Sex Roles* 32: 159–167.

New York Division of Human Rights. 1993. "Survey of the Costs of Sexual Harassment." Reported in J. Avner, Chairperson, *Sexual Harassment: Building a Consensus for Change.* Final Report Submitted to Governor Mario Cuomo, Albany, NY.

Petrocelli, W., and B. Repa. 1995. *Sexual Harassment on the Job: What It Is and How to Stop It.* Berkeley, CA: Nolo Press.

Russell, D. 1984. *Sexual Exploitation: Rape, Child Sexual Abuse, and Workplace Harassment.* Beverly Hills, CA: Sage.

Salisbury, J., A. Ginoria, H. Remick, and D. Stringer. 1986. "Counseling Victims of Sexual Harassment. *Psychotherapy* 23: 316–324.

Shattuck, C., and K. Williams. 1992. *Employer's Guide to Controlling Sexual Harassment.* Washington: Thompson.

Solotoff, L., and H. Kramer. 1994. *Sex Discrimination and Sexual Harassment in the Workplace.* New York: Law Journal Seminars Press.

Stringer, D., H. Remick, J. Salisbury, and A. Ginorio. 1990. "The Power and Reasons Behind Sexual Harassment: An Employer's Guide to Solutions. *Public Personnel Management* 19: 43–52.

Sumrall, A., and D. Taylor, eds. 1992. *Sexual Harassment: Women Speak Out.* Freedom, CA: Crossing Press.

Tangri, S., M. Burt, and L. Johnson. 1982. "Sexual Harassment at Work: Three Explanatory Models. *Journal of Social Issues* 38: 33–54.

U.S. Merit Systems Protection Board. 1981. *Sexual Harassment of Federal Workers: Is It a Problem?* Washington, DC: U.S. Government Printing Office.

———. 1987. *Sexual Harassment of Federal Workers: An Update*. Washington, DC: U.S. Government Printing Office.

SEXUAL HARASSMENT ON COLLEGE CAMPUSES

Adams, J., J. Kottke, and J. Padgitt. 1983. "Sexual Harassment of University Students. *Journal of College Student Personnel* 24: 484–490.

Bailey, N., and M. Richards. August 1985. "Tarnishing the Ivory Tower: Sexual Harassment in Graduate Training Programs." Paper presented at the Annual Meeting of the American Psychological Association, Los Angeles, CA.

Barickman, R. B., M. A. Paludi, and V. C. Rabinowitz. 1992. "Sexual Harassment of Students: Victims of the College Experience. In *Victimization: An International Perspective*. Edited by E. Viano. New York: Springer.

DeChiara, P. 1988. "The Need for Universities to Have Rules on Consensual Relationships Between Faculty and Students. *Columbia Journal of Law and Social Problems* 21: 137–162.

DeFour, D. C. 1990. "The Interface of Racism and Sexism on College Campuses." In *Ivory Power: Sexual Harassment on campus*. Edited by M. A. Paludi. Albany: State University of New York Press.

Dietz-Uhler, B., and A. Murrell. 1992. "College Students' Perceptions of Sexual Harassment: Are Gender Differences Decreasing? *Journal of College Student Development* 33: 540–546.

Dziech, B., and L. Weiner. 1984. *The Lecherous Professor*. Boston: Beacon Press.

Fitzgerald, L. F., Y. Gold, and K. Brock. 1990. "Responses to Victimization: Validation of an Objective Policy." *Journal of College Student Personnel* 27: 34–39.

Fitzgerald, L. F., and A. Omerod. 1993. "Sexual Harassment in Academia and the Workplace." In *Psychology of Women: Handbook of Issues and Theories.* Edited by F. L. Denmark and M. A. Paludi. Westport, CT: Greenwood.

Fitzgerald, L. F., S. Shullman, N. Bailey, M. Richards, J. Swecker, Y. Gold, A. Omerod, and L. Weitzman. 1988. "The Incidence and Dimensions of Sexual Harassment in Academia and the Workplace. *Journal of Vocational Behavior* 32: 152–175.

Keller, E. 1990. Consensual Relationships and Institutional Policy. *Academe* 76: 29–32.

Kenig, S., and J. Ryan. 1986. "Sex Differences in Levels of Tolerance and Attribution of Blame for Sexual Harassment on a University Campus. *Sex Roles* 15: 535–549.

Koss, M. P. 1990. "Changed Lives: The Psychological Impact of Sexual Harassment. In *Ivory Power: Sexual Harassment on Campus.* Edited by M. A. Paludi. Albany: State University of New York Press.

Lott, B. 1993. "Sexual Harassment: Consequences and Realities. *NEA Higher Education Journal* 8: 89–103.

Lott, B., and M. E. Reilly, eds. 1996. *Combatting Sexual Harassment in Higher Education.* Washington, DC: NEA Professional Library.

Malovich, N. J., and J. E. Stake. 1990. "Sexual Harassment of Women on Campus: Individual Differences in Attitude and Belief. *Psychology of Women Quarterly* 14: 63–81.

Paludi, M. A., ed. 1990. *Ivory Power: Sexual Harassment on Campus.* Albany: State University of New York Press.

———. 1996. *Sexual Harassment on College Campuses: Abusing the Ivory Power.* Albany: State University of New York Press.

Project on the Status and Education of Women. 1978. *Sexual Harassment: A Hidden Issue.* Washington, DC: Association of American Colleges.

Quina, K. 1996. "Sexual Harassment and Rape: A Continuum of Exploitation." In *Ivory Power: Sexual Harassment on Campus*. Edited by M. A. Paludi. Albany: State University of New York Press.

Rabinowitz, V. C. 1990. "Coping with Sexual Harassment." In *Ivory Power: Sexual Harassment on Campus*. Edited by M. A. Paludi. Albany: State University of New York Press.

Reilly, M., B. Lott, and S. Gallogly. 1986. "Sexual Harassment of University Students." *Sex Roles* 15: 333–358.

Sandler, B., L. Silverberg, and R. Hall. 1996. *The Chilly Classroom Climate: A Guide to Improve the Education of Women*. Washington, DC: National Association for Women in Education.

Schneider, B. 1987. "Graduate Women, Sexual Harassment, and University Policy." *Journal of Higher Education* 58: 46–65.

Stites, M. C. 1996. "Consensual Relationships." In *Sexual Harassment on College Campuses: Abusing the Ivory Power*. Edited by M. A. Paludi. Albany: State University of New York Press.

Zalk, S. R. 1990. "Men in the Academy: A Psychological Profile of Harassment." In *Ivory Power: Sexual Harassment on Campus*. Edited by M. A. Paludi. Albany: State University of New York Press.

Zalk, S. R., M. A. Paludi, and J. Dederich. 1991. "Women Students' Assessment of Consensual Relationships with Their Professors: Ivory Power Reconsidered." In *Academic and Workplace Sexual Harassment: A Resource Manual*. Edited by M. A. Paludi and R. B. Barickman. Albany: State University of New York Press.

SEXUAL HARASSMENT IN ELEMENTARY AND SECONDARY SCHOOLS

American Association of University Women. 1993. *Hostile Hallways*. Washington, DC: Author.

Ben Tsvi-Mayer, S., R. Hertz-Lazarowitz, and M. Safir. 1980. "Teachers' Selections of Boys and Girls as Prominent Pupils." *Sex Roles* 21: 231–245.

Bogart, K., S. Simmons, N. Stein, and E. Tomaszewski. 1992. "Breaking the Silence: Sexual and Gender-based Harassment in elementary, Secondary, and Postsecondary Education." In *Sex Equity and Sexuality in Education*. Edited by S. Klein. Albany: State University of New York Press.

Chamberlain, E. October 1994. "Power, Consent, and Adolescent Sexual Harassment." Paper presented at the Meeting of the Northeastern Educational Research Association, Ellenville, NY.

Corbett, K. 1993. "Sexual Harassment in High School." *Youth and Society* 25: 93–103.

Feltey, K. 1991. "Sexual Coercion Attitudes Among High School Students: The Influence of Gender and Rape Education." *Youth and Society* 23: 229–250.

Larkin, J. 1994. "Walking Through Walls: The Sexual Harassment of High School Girls." *Gender and Education* 6: 263–280.

Layman, N. 1994. *Sexual Harassment in American Secondary Schools: A Legal Guide for Administrators, Teachers, and Students*. Dallas, TX: Contemporary Research Press.

Linn, E., N. Stein, J. Young, and S. Davis. 1992. "Bitter Lessons for All: Sexual Harassment in Schools." In *Sexuality and the Curriculum*. Edited by J. Sears. New York: Teachers College Press.

Phinney, G. S. 1994. "Sexual Harassment: A Dynamic Element in the Lives of Middle School Girls and Teachers. *Equity and Excellence in Education* 27: 5–10.

Roscoe, B. 1994. "Sexual Harassment: An Educational Program for Middle School Students. *Elementary School Guidance and Counseling* 29: 110–120.

Roscoe, B. 1994. "Sexual Harassment: Early Adolescents' Self-reports of Experiences and Acceptance." *Adolescence* 29: 515–523.

Stein, N. 1993. "Secrets in Public: Sexual Harassment in Public and Private Schools." Working Paper, Wellesley College, No. 256.

———. April 1994. "Seeing Is Not Believing: Sexual Harassment in Public School and the Role of Adults." Paper presented at the Annual Meeting of the American Educational Research Association, New Orleans, LA.

Turner, P. 1995. "Sensitivity to Verbally and Physically Harassing Behaviors and Incidents in Junior High/Middle School Students." Master's thesis, Fort Hays State University.

Wickum, B. 1992. "Sexual Harassment in School: Protecting Students From Their Peers." *Journal of Intergroup Relations* 19: 13–18.

Surveys on Sexual Harassment

ATTITUDES TOWARD VICTIM BLAME
AND VICTIM RESPONSIBILITY

Source: Michele Paludi and Associates,
Consultants in Sexual Harassment

Directions: For each of the following statements, indicate whether you agree or disagree, using the following scale:

    1: disagree strongly
    2: disagree
    3: neutral—neither agree nor disagree
    4: agree
    5: agree strongly

1. A sexually harassed woman is a desirable woman.
2. The extent of the woman's resistance to harassment should be the major factor in determining if harassment has occurred.
3. A sexually harassed woman is usually an innocent victim.
4. Women often claim sexual harassment to protect their reputations.

5. Any woman may be sexually harassed.
6. Many women claim sexual harassment if they have consented to sexual relations but have changed their minds afterwards.
7. A woman should not blame herself for sexual harassment.
8. A woman can successfully resist a harasser if she really tries.
9. Sexually experienced women are not really damaged by sexual harassment.
10. Many women invent sexual harassment stories if they learn they are failing a course.
11. It would do some women good to be sexually harassed.
12. Women who are good students are as likely to be sexually harassed as women who are bad students.
13. Women do not provoke sexual harassment by their appearance or behavior.
14. Men, not women, are responsible for sexual harassment.
15. Women put themselves in situations in which they are likely to be sexually harassed because they have an unconscious wish to be harassed.
16. In most cases, when a woman is sexually harassed, she deserved it.
17. Virtually all women who have reported sexual harassment are able to rebuild their careers and their belief in their own competence.
18. Sexual harassment is not innocent flirtation and women are not flattered by the behavior.

FACULTY-STUDENT INTERACTIONS

Source: Michele Paludi & Associates,
Consultants in Sexual Harassment

Instructions: You will see a series of questions dealing with faculty/instructor-student interactions on college campuses.

We are interested in your perceptions of the frequency of occurrence of a variety of interactions. For each item, please circle the number which most closely describes your best guess of the incidence of each type of interaction described. We are not interested in your actual observations or reports of specifice events—just your perceptions. If you circle a 2 or 3, please indicate whether you guess the professors/instructors involved are only women, only men, or involve both women and men by circling F, M, or B, respectively.

Key:

Perceived Frequency:

1: Never
2: Infrequently or a rarely isolated event
3: A fairly regular or common event

Sex(es) of professors involved:

F: Female
M: Male
B: Both female and male

1. A professor/instructor invites undergraduate students to participate in ongoing research projects.

   1 2 3   F M B

2. A professor/instructor lends books or journal articles to a student for independent projects.

   1 2 3   F M B

3. A professor/instructor raises an exam score after discussing the exam with a student.

   1 2 3   F M B

4. A professor/instructor lowers an exam score after discussing the exam with a student.

   1 2 3   F M B

5. A professor/instructor tells suggestive stories or offensive jokes to students in class.

   1 2 3   F M B

6. A professor/instructor makes crude sexual remarks, either publicly in class or to students privately.

    1 2 3   F M B

7. A professor/instructor publishes a paper with an undergraduate student as coauthor.

    1 2 3   F M B

8. A professor/instructor writes a letter of recommendation for a student's application to a graduate program.

    1 2 3   F M B

9. A professor/instructor makes seductive remarks about women's appearance, bodies, or sexual activities.

    1 2 3   F M B

10. A professor/instructor uses sexist teaching materials in classes.

    1 2 3   F M B

11. A professor/instructor deprecates women students in the class.

    1 2 3   F M B

12. A professor/instructor gives students an extension on a term paper.

    1 2 3   F M B

13. A professor/instructor asks a student to babysit for their children.

    1 2 3   F M B

14. A professor/instructor dates a student in a current class.

    1 2 3   F M B

15. A professor/instructor dates a former student.

    1 2 3   F M B

16. A professor/instructor has a cup of coffee with a student in the college cafeteria.

1 2 3   F M B

17. A professor/instructor has a drink with a student in a pub nearby campus.

1 2 3   F M B

18. A professor/instructor presents a paper with a student at a professional conference.

1 2 3   F M B

19. A professor/instructor offers a student some sort of reward for being sexually cooperative.

1 2 3   F M B

20. A professor/instructor lends students money to get home for spring break.

1 2 3   F M B

21. A professor/instructor makes unwanted attempts to touch or fondle a student.

1 2 3   F M B

22. A professor/instructor asks a student to type and do other clerical work in their office.

1 2 3   F M B

23. A professor/instructor threatens a student with some sort of punishment for not being sexually cooperative.

1 2 3   F M B

24. A professor/instructor gives a student an incomplete in a college course.

1 2 3   F M B

25. A professor/instructor sexually harasses a student.

1 2 3   F M B

26. A professor/instructor mentors a college student.

1 2 3   F M B

APPENDIX II

Sexual Harassment Law:
Resources and Remedies

Introduction

All sexual harassment is illegal, from offensive sexist remarks and pornography displayed in the workplace to sexual assault (including rape). But statutes on paper are useless unless we know how to make them work for us.

The first head of the Equal Opportunity Employment Commission (EEOC), the agency charged with enforcement of Title VII of the Civil Rights Act, treated the provisions against sexual discrimination as a joke, saying that it was "conceived out of wedlock" (Petrocelli and Repa 1995, 18). And, in fact, conservative opponents of the Civil Rights Bill had introduced the amendment adding discrimination on the basis of sex to the bill in the belief that a clause so preposterous would make passage of the bill impossible. Pressure from women's groups eventually forced the EEOC to take action against job discrimination based on sex. But federal courts continued to treat claims of sexual harassment as a personal matter between the employee and the harasser. It was not until 1980, when Eleanor Holmes Norton headed the EEOC, that the commission issued guidelines defining sexual harassment and declaring it a form of sex discrimination prohibited by Title VII.

In 1981, complaints of sexual harassment, exactly 3,661, were filed with the EEOC, more than the total filed in the previous decade. By 1990, the number of complaints had increased more than 50 percent to 5,694. In 1991, during the three months following Anita Hill's testimony that Supreme Court nominee, now Supreme Court Justice Clarence Thomas had sexually harassed her, the EEOC reported a 70 percent increase in claims filed compared with the same period in 1990. The increase in the number of claims following public awareness of the impact and pervasiveness of sexual harassment continues.

Given recent Supreme Court decisions and rulings in lower federal courts and state courts, the legitimacy of statutes against sexual harassment seems unassailable. Individuals each year are given relief from sexual harassment where they work or study and often receive monetary compensation and restoration of job or academic losses. Individuals who have sexually harassed their coworkers are identified, restrained, and often sanctioned. We should not minimize the importance of this legal remedy for those who have suffered the abuse of sexual harassment and have had the courage to file successful legal claims. Yet when we compare the incidence of sexual harassment in the workplace, where studies have consistently found close to 90 percent of women reporting personal experience of sexual harassment, to the number of women filing claims together with the number of women filing civil suits for damages, it is clear that far less then 1 percent of the incidents of sexual harassment that occur each year receive legal remedy. Considering the extent of the problem and the manifold ways in which it is woven into the texture of everyday life (comparable to racism), we must acknowledge that the greatest power of sexual harassment law is as a mandate and a restraining force.

In order for policies to be effective in providing working and learning environments free of sexual harassment, however, it is crucial for those charged with developing and enforcing policies to be thoroughly aware of what constitutes sexual harassment under the law (state and local, as well as federal). And this is certainly a more complex matter than simply listing and quoting the EEOC definition of sexual harassment. Counselors, administrators, executives, managers, personnel directors, and employee assistance programs personnel all need a detailed, accurate, and up-to-date knowledge of the law. As far as possible, the essential legal principles that underlie sexual harassment policies need to be shared with those protected by such policies—as well as those who are likely to violate them. In this appendix, we will provide a brief introduction to this information. We recommend consulting with attorneys as well as the following texts for more detailed information:

Levy, A., and M. A. Paludi. 1997. *Workplace Sexual Harassment.* Englewood Cliffs, NJ: Prentice Hall.

Petrocelli, W., and B. Repa. 1995. *Sexual Harassment on the Job: What It Is and How to Stop It.* Berkeley, CA: Nolo Press.

Shattuck, C., and K. Williams. 1992. *Employer's Guide to Controlling Sexual Harassment.* Washington: Thompson.

Solotoff, L., and H. Kramer. 1994. *Sex Discrimination and Sexual Harassment in the Workplace.* New York: Law Journal Seminars Press.

LEGAL FOUNDATIONS

Federal Statutes and Case Law

All federal law on sexual harassment—both statutory and case law—rests on Title VII of the Civil Rights Act of 1964. Title IX of the Education Amendments of 1972 is essentially an extension (with some modifications) of Title VII to educational institutions that receive federal funds, including students as well as employees. Most states have civil rights legislation which deals with sexual harassment in businesses within those states, and most of this legislation is also modeled on Title VII. Furthermore, state courts often use federal cases as precedents for interpretation of their own state statutes.

Guidelines issued by the Equal Employment Opportunity Commission (EEOC) in 1980 set the primary standard for implementing the provisions of Title VII. These guidelines define the various forms sexual harassment can take more explicitly, and provide a basis for a number of court decisions since 1980 that have gradually extended the range of the protections offered under Title VII. These guidelines are also the basis for most policies against sexual harassment that have been established by academic institutions and businesses; they are frequently quoted in brochures and policy statements. Sexual harassment is defined as "unwelcome sexual advances, requests for sexual favors, and other verbal or physical conduct of a sexual nature" that constitute sexual harassment when:

> submission to the conduct is either explicitly or implicitly a term or condition of an individual's employment; or submission to or rejection of such conduct by an individual is used as the basis for employment decisions affecting that individual; and/or such conduct has the purpose or effect of unreasonably interfering with an individual's work performance or creating an intimidating or hostile work environment.

In 1981 the Office of Civil Rights (OCR) of the U.S. Department of Education adopted these guidelines as their interpretation of Title IXs prohibitions against sexual harassment and extended their range to cover academic standing, academic performance, and learning environment.

The OCR's definition stipulates: "Sexual harassment consists of verbal or physical conduct of a sexual nature, imposed on the basis of sex, by an employee or agent of a recipient of federal funds that denies, limits, provides different, or otherwise conditions the provision of aid, benefits, services, or treatment protected under Title IX." The OCR definition does suggest the comprehensive range of offensive behavior covered by its interpretation of Title IX, appropriately stressing harmful sex-differential treatment as the governing principle rather than the more familiar (and mistaken) idea that harassing sexual behavior must be motivated by the desire for personal sexual gratification.

The legal status of these definitions has been supported by a number of court decisions, most notably the 1986 Supreme Court decision in *Meritor Savings Bank v. Vinson*. The court unanimoulsy affirmed that "sexual harassment claims are not limited simply to those for which a tangible job benefit is witheld ('quid pro quo' sexual harassment), but also include those in which a complainant is subjected to an offensive, discriminatory work environment ('hostile environment' sexual harassment" (Bennett-Alexander 1987, 65). Since an individual who submits to sexual demands under threat of job loss or other intimidation may indeed receive apparent rewards and priviliges (as Mechelle Vinson did), this Supreme Court decision establishes a standard of accountability that is extremely important. If adopted by colleges and universities, for example, the "hostile environment" provision would cover the most pervasive form of sexual harassment of students, experienced by as many as 85 percent of women students: "gender harassment" (generalized sexist speech and behavior, Paludi 1996).

The history of litigation under Title VII of the 1964 Civil Rights Act dates back only twenty-five years. In the early 1970s, when the first cases were heard, the courts refused to recognize even physically offensive behavior (such as patting, grabbing, and pinching) by supervisors and coworkers as actionable sexual harassment. They held that this was "an innocent intrusion of sexual by-play into the workplace," or, even if harm was clearly sustained, the courts generally did not find employers responsible unless they directly knew of and condoned such behavior (Lindgren and Taub, 1988, 169). In other words, the courts did not recognize a positive responsibility on the part of employers for providing a workplace environment free of sexual harassment (even though such responsibility was recognized by that time in regard to racial discrimination prohibited by the same statute).

In 1977 a case argued before the United States Court of Appeals, Tompkins v. Public Service Electric and Gas, provided a new and substantially more progressive direction. Adrienne Tomkins, who was employed as a secretary by PSE&G, was sexually harassed by her supervisor, who made verbal and physical sexual advances and indicated that her agreement to have sex with him was a necessary condition for a favorable evaluation. She reported this behavior to appropriate officals within the company and was promised a transfer to a comparable position. Instead, she was transferred to an inferior position, was given false and adverse employment evaluations, disciplinary layoffs, and threats of demotion by other supervisors. A little more than a year after the incident, Tompkins was fired and subsequently filed a complaint with the EEOC.

The court ruled in Tompkins' favor, holding that the conditions necessary for finding a violation of Title VII were present: "a term or condition of employment had been imposed . . . in a sexually discriminatory fashion"; and the employer did not take "prompt and appropriate remedial action" after being informed of the circumstances (Lindgren and Taub 1988, 171). The standard of employer accountability had been substantially strengthened.

In Bundy v. Jackson the United States Court of Appeals for the District of Columbia (1981) found that the complainant, Sandra Bundy, had sustained harm under Title VII's provisions, even though there was no evidence of a "quid pro quo" loss. Bundy was propositioned by a coworker, then by two supervisors, one of whom frequently summoned her to his office to ask her to have sex with him and to question her about her sexual preferences. When she complained to their supervisor, he casually dismissed her complaints, telling her that "any man in his right mind would want to rape you," and pressured her to have sex with him. Chief Judge J. Skelly Wright strongly affirmed that a hostile sexual environment was intolerable and illegal in and of itself:

We thus readily conclude that Bundy's employer dis-
criminaged against her on the basis of sex. . . . Sexual
harassment of the sort Bundy suffered amounted by
itself to sex discrimination with respect to the "terms,
conditions, or privileges of employment."

In 1991 the Ninth Circuit Court of Appeals found "hostile environment" discrimination in a situation involving a
much less obviously abusive work environment and, in the
process, extended substantially the conception of an
employer's responsibility to protect employees from sexual
harassment. The case, *Ellison v. Brady*, involved the
"romantic overtures" of one employee to another, expressed
through notes and persistent requests. While the district
court considered this behavior "trivial and isolated"—in
effect, part of the ordinary working environment—the Court
of Appeals found that a hostile enviroment had indeed
existed and had been tolerated by the employer. The court's
judgment gives no definitive set of conditions that constitute
hostile environment sexual harassment. In fact, the decision
states: "Our examples are illustrative and not exclusive
because we realize that sexual harassment is a rapidly
expanding area of the law." Instead the decision suggests
what most experts in the field of sexual harassment prevention have maintained; employers and their agents should
give considerable weight to an individual's claim that she
has experienced sexual harassment and should not prejudge
a situation according to a set of criteria that may be too limited or outmoded (Levy and Paludi 1997).

In 1993, a unanimous decision by the Supreme Court
clarified and substantially broadened the protections
against a hostile sexual environment, reversing the lower
courts' ruling that, absent demonstrated psychological
injury or loss in job performance, a claim of offensive, hostile, or intimidating sexual harassment could not be sustained (*Harris v. Forklift Systems*). The Supreme Court
rejected this argument, finding that "no single factor is
required" to prove a "hostile environment" sexual harassment claim. Justice O'Connor wrote:

Title VII comes into play before the harassing conduct leads to a nervous breakdown. A discriminatorily abusive work environment, even one that does not seriously affect employees' psychological well-being, can and often will detract from employees' job performance, discourage employees from remaining on the job, or keep them from advancing in their careers. Moreover . . . the very fact that the discriminatory conduct was so severe or pervasive that it created a work environment abusive to employees because of their . . . gender offends Title VII's broad rule of workplace equality.

In 1991, a federal judge permitted the first class action suit charging hostile environment sexual harassment (*Jensen v. Evelith Taconite Co.*). The court ruled, after trial, that Evelith mines discriminated against the entire class of women miners who brought the suit "by maintaining an environment sexually hostile to women." The judge cited numerous forms of unwanted and offensive sexual behavior: graffiti, photos, cartoons, verbal statements and language reflecting a sexualized, male-oriented environment, and anti-female environment," and "physical acts that reflected a sexual motive or concern." The judge stated: "In work places which have been traditionaly male and where females constitute a small minority of the employees, employers may have an increased obligation to create environments which are safe for all employees."

Subsequently, the Supreme Court substantially extended the range of sanctions under Title IX. The OCR of the Department of Education has established that Title IX provides the same protections as Title VII, for students as well as employees. The Civil Rights Restoration Act of 1988 guarantees these provisions to all members of academic institutions that receive federal funds (not just to those areas of the institution actually receiving the funds, as the Supreme Court had held in *Grove City College v. Bell* (in 1984). The only remedy provided until recently, however, was withdrawal of federal funds from an institution that violates the provisions against sexual harassment. And to this date, no college or university has lost federal funds for failure to protect students or employees against sexual harassment. Thus, students had little incentive to bring legal action against a school or college even when the institution had acknowledged the sexual harassment. Title IX provides no monetary damages or direct restitution of losses the student may have suffered (lowering of grades, damage to career, inability to complete an educational program, and physical and emotional trauma).

In 1992, the Supreme Court, in an unanimous ruling, upheld the suit of a high school student, Christine Franklin, against her high school. She claimed that the school had failed to protect her against persistent sexual harassment by a male teacher, harassment that included rape. A federal trial court had dismissed the case, stating that she could not sue for damages under Title IX. The Supreme Court ruled that she could sue for damages and did not limit the amount she could be awarded.

This ruling is especially significant because, in contrast to the case history of Title VII litigation, there have not been many lawsuits brought against colleges and universities under Title IX (Watts 1996). Until *Franklin v. Gwinett County Public Schools*, the only circuit court decision on the sexual harassment of students, *Alexander v. Yale University*, 1980, seemed to support the district court's conclusion that "the concept of mere *respondeat superior* appears ill-adapted to the question of Title IX sex discrimination based on harassment incidents" (Lindgren and Taub 1988, 301). This concept holds a principal liable for the actions of his or her agent, so the court's conclusion indicates that an academic institution could not ordinarily be held accountable when an instructor or other employee harassed a student unless some specific negligence could be shown. *Franklin v. Gwinett County Public Schools*, in effect, reversed that opinion and extended protections to students comparable to those established under Title VII for employees.

STATE LAW

State labor laws have changed dramatically to include sexual harassment as a major concern. Nearly all state fair employment practices statutes (FEP) prohibit sex discrimination and base their legal remedies upon Title VII (even when they do not explictly refer to sexual harassment). The EEOC and most state FEP agencies cooperate to avoid duplication of work. If an FEP is "designated" by the EEOC, it must meet standards set by the federal agency in staffing, funding, and enforcement. The EEOC and designated agencies often work closely together, accepting each other's investigations of cases and referring cases to eath other. Most states have a dual-filing agreement with the EEOC, so that a case filed under one agency is automatically filed under the other.

State legislatures have been exploring new approaches to deal with and contain sexual harassment. Alaska, California, Illinois, Minnesota, Tennessee, Vermont, and Washington now require employers to post notices informing employees that sexual harassment is illegal and telling them what to do if they are harassed. Illinois now requires all businesses with state contracts to have written sexual harassment policies; Iowa has enacted a comprehensive prohibition that covers state employees, people in the care or custody of the state, and students. California, Connecticut, Illinois, Tennessee, and Vermont require employers to conduct training sessions on the nature and prevention of sexual harassment. A number of other states, California, Connecticut, Iowa, Minnesota, New Hampshire, Tennessee, and Washington, require all state educational institutions to take various steps against sexual harassment, including the formulation of policies and disciplinary procedures.

In most instances Title VII applies only to businesses with fifteen or more employees, but many state laws dealing with sexual harassment cover smaller businesses. In Michigan, for example, all businesses are covered; Connecticut's FEP statutes include companies with three or more employees; Iowa's cover companies with four or more employees. As a result, most businesses today are covered by one or more statutes—federal, state, and frequently local.

FILING A CLAIM WITH THE EEOC

We recommend the reader become familiar with filing a claim with the EEOC by reading chapter 1 in this book. Additional resources include:

Levy, A., and M. A. Paludi. 1997. *Workplace Sexual Harassment.* Englewood Cliffs, NJ: Prentice Hall.

Petrocelli, W., and B. Repa. 1995. *Sexual Harassment on the Job: What It Is and How to Stop It.* Berkeley, CA: Nolo Press.

Shattuck, C., and K. Williams. 1992. *Employer's Guide to Controlling Sexual Harassment.* Washington: Thompson.

Solotoff, L., and H. Kramer. 1994. *Sex Discrimination and Sexual Harassment in the Workplace.* New York: Law Journal Seminars Press.

FILING A CLAIM UNDER FEP STATUTES

Although state FEP laws vary considerably in their provisions and their effectiveness, their procedures are usually similar to the EEOC's. The requirements for filing a claim and the agencies' methods and powers of investigation are generally based on EEOC guidelines. Most FEP agencies have been "designated" by the EEOC—essentially meaning certified— and most cooperate with the EEOC to share the work load and to avoid duplication of investigative procedures.

Through the dual-filing agreements the EEOC maintains with most of the designated FEP agencies, a claim filed with one of the two agencies is automatically filed with the other.

All designated FEP agencies have the power to stop ongoing sexual harassment. They can also provide assistance in recovering lost wages and other job-related losses.

About half the state agencies have only these minimum powers. In other states, the FEP statutes provide monetary damages, often greater than those permitted under Title VII. Although state FEP statutes typically establish a minimum number of employees that a business must have before it is covered, these minimums are never more than and often much less than the fifteen employee minimum of Title VII. Several state FEP laws provide administrative hearings as an alternative to lawsuits (for example, California, Connecticut, Illinois, and New York). The state often provides an attorney or pays the fees of an attorney and often awards monetary damages. If an employee files a claim in a state with these provisions, he/she may find it faster, simpler, and less expensive to take advantage of this process than filing a lawsuit. In some states, one must file a claim with an FEP agency before filing a private lawsuit.

A NOTE ON LOCAL LAWS AND AGENCIES

Many cities and counties have laws prohibiting sexual harassment and agencies to enforce them, often modeled on EEOC or FEP agencies. The local EEOC or FEP agency should be able to provide information on whether such a local agency exists. It may be advantagous to file with a local agency in addition to claims with the EEOC and FEP offices. Local laws may not have restrictions—or not such rigorous restrictions—on the minimum number of employees a covered business must have. Local ordinances may define sexual harassment more inclusively than federal or state law (for example, specifying sexual orientation as a protected category). They may also allow compensatory and/or punitive damages even when state FEP statutes do not.

USING CIVIL LAW SUITS (COMMON LAW TORTS)

Whether or not an employee has filed claims of sexual harassment under Title VII of the U.S. Civil Rights Act, state Fair Employment Practices statutes, or city or county ordinances, he/she is entitled to sue to recover damages (file a tort action) under all states' civil laws. Tort claims are filed in state courts like any other personal injury suit. The grounds for these actions include assault and battery, and defamation. A successful suit may award compensatory damages for emotional and physical distress suffered as a result of the harassment and punitive damages as well.

A tort action may be filed in conjunction with other claims filed with state, local, and federal agencies. In certain circumstance, it may be the best—or only—course of action. If an individual is employed by a small business not covered by Title VII or FEP statutes—or if state laws allow insufficient damages—a tort action may be the only way to achieve compensation. Many state laws provide only compensation for lost wages, and sometimes medical expenses. Few provide punitive damages or damages for stress-related ailments. If the filing limits set by the EEOC and state FEP agencies have expired, tort action may again be the only recourse.

Because there are no limits on damages that can be awarded in common law tort actions, an employee may be able to receive much larger compensatory and punitive damages from a civil suit than state or federal laws allow. If fewer than 100 employees work for an employer, for example, the total allowable award is $50,000. A civil suit is especially worth considering if the employee can demonstrate severe suffering and impairment from the trauma of sexual harassment.

Tort Actions often Filed against Sexual Harassers

Assault and Battery. To prove an assault occurred, the employee must demonstrate that the person who assaulted him/her intended to cause physical harm and that this harmful contact was feared. In some cases, verbal threats and menacing gestures may constitute assault. Battery is actual physical contact that is harmful, offensive, or insulting. The person accused of battery must have intended to touch the complainaint and must have made physical contact. Note that the physical contact need not cause physical harm to constitute battery; it may be offensive or insulting and may include, in the case of sexual harassment: kissing, embracing, touching in an offensive way, and rubbing against another's body.

Intentional Infliction of Emotional Distress. This is the most common tort action filed as a result of sexual harassment and the one likely to secure monetary damages for emotional trauma and suffering. The employee must be able to prove that: (*a*) the harasser behaved outrageously and intentionally caused emotional distress (or should have known that the actions would cause distress); and (*b*) that the employee suffered severe emotional trauma as a result of the harasser's conduct.

"Emotional distress" has proved to be a particularly difficult concept for courts to define. The courts usually require some evidence that the emotional distress has caused physical symptoms such as sleep disorders, severe headaches, skin rashes, or psychological symptoms attested to by a physician or therapist. Medical records are very important evidence.

Defamation. To support a common law tort claim of defamation, the employee must show that the person who defamed her/him made a false or damaging statement about her/him; told or wrote that statement to at least one other person; and intended to harm her/him through that statement—or was negligent in making it. Further, the employee must demonstrate that the communication harmed him/her in some way, causing the loss of a job or promotion, for instance, or causing other people to avoid contact with or to express unfavorable opinions about him/her.

Actions alleging slander often conflict with constitutional protections of freedom of speech. People have the right to express opinions, even derogatory, malicious, and hurtful gossip. In seeking to find a middle ground between these competing legal interests, courts have generally held that statements are defamatory in the workplace if they are false claims that an employee behaved in some way that would clearly make him/her unfit for her job (abused drugs or alcohol, committed a crime, performed her duties incompetently).

As with every instance of sexual harassment it is important—sometimes crucial—to keep a precise record of exactly what was said, date and time, witnesses, and so forth, to support a claim.

Invasion of Privacy. Often referred to by the more specific term "intrusion," this tort action claims that an individual's privacy was violated. The complainant need not demonstrate emotional trauma or even, in most courts, physical entry into a place where the intruder is clearly unwelcome. Courts now tend to recognize that harassing phone calls, following a coworker outside the workplace, and inappropriate questions about sexual behavior or preferences may all constitute illegal intrusion. An Alabama court held, for instance, that a person's "emotional sanctum is certainly due the same expectations of privacy as one's physical environment." (The case involved an employer who regularly pestered a woman with questions about her sex life and demanded that she have sex with him.) (Petrocelli and Repa 1995, 8).

Wrongful Discharge. An employee who has been fired illegally may be able to sue the employer for wrongful discharge. If successful, the employee may receive compensation not only for lost wages but also for any other injury, such as mental distress, suffered because of loss of employment. In the past, the legal doctrine of "employment at will" made it nearly impossible to win a suit for wrongful discharge. Under this doctrine, most employees are considered to be "employees at will" (the will of the employer), who may be fired for any legal reason. Because of court rulings during the past decade, however, most states recognize an important exception that enables sexually harassed employees, who have been fired, to successfully file a claim of wrongful discharge. In nearly every state, courts have held that an employee cannot be legally fired for refusing to tolerate conduct that violates public policy— and Title VII and FEP statutes prohibiting sexual harassment on the job have clearly established such a policy.

Rape. Most people, unfortunately, continue to view rape as a different phenomenon from sexual harassment. Petrocelli and Repa (1995) refer to rape as "the most outrageous and egregious form of workplace harassment" (p.23). Given the continuum of acts of sexual harassment from generalized sexist remarks to rape, it is not surprising that the trauma usually experienced by women who have been raped is also experienced in various forms and degrees by women subjected to less violent and abusive forms of harassment.

Rape is a criminal offense in all states, of course, and rapists are prosecuted in criminal courts. It is also possible for a woman raped by a coworker or supervisor to file a tort claim for damages. State laws and court judgments have moved away from the demand for proofs that the rapist used violence or the threat of bodily injury to a more realistic recognition of the nature of rape, where coercion and terrorization need not involve the use of physical force. Although most state laws still require proof that some force was used during a rape, courts usually include verbal threats within this category. In a few states, no proof of force is required. Wisconsin statutes, for example, includes within the category of third-degree assault sexual intercourse with a woman who has not given her consent, even if there is no open resistance or use of force (Petrocelli and Repa 1995, 24). We recommend reading the references listed above for further discussion of torts.

LEGAL RESOURCES AND REMEDIES FOR STUDENTS

In 1981, the Office of Civil Rights of the U.S. Department of Education (OCR) adopted the guidelines on sexual harassment developed by the EEOC and extended them, under Title IX of the Education Amendments of 1972, to cover students' academic standing, academic performance, and learning environment. The OCR has held that Title IX offers the same protections to students that Title VII provides for employees. The Civil Rights Restoration Act of 1988 guarantees its provisions to all members of academic institutions that receive federal funds, not just to those areas of these institutions that receive federal funds directly, as the Supreme Court had held in *Grove City College v. Bell*, 1984. (Of course, students who are employed by these institutions and all other employees there are fully covered by the provisions of Title VII we have previously discussed.) In early 1997, OCR issued a sexual harassment guidance that details components of an effective policy statement and investigatory procedures. We recommend consulting this guidance for additional information. This guidance may be obtained by phoning 1-800-421-3481.

Until recently, however, the only remedy Title IX provided was withdrawal of federal funds from an institution found to violate the provisions against sexual harassment (or other forms of discrimination). This drastic, wholesale penalty has, predictably, never been applied to any academic institutions and no school, college, or university has ever lost federal funds for failure to protect students or employees against sexual harassment. (In sharp contrast to the judgments against companies and corporations under Title VII for failure to protect employees from sexual harassment.

One reason for this record of inaction is the lack of incentive provided by Title IX for students to file a complaint with the OCR when they have been sexually harassed. There is no provision for monetary damages or direct restitution of losses the student has suffered (such as damage to career, lowering of grades, inability to complete an educational program, and physical and emotional trauma). Students are only temporarily members of an academic community and generally have less incentive to endure the risks of filing charges of sexual harassment than do employees whose livelihood depends on their jobs and who frequently can change employers only with considerable financial hardship (if at all). Students also typically have some mobility within the academic institution, especially in colleges, and may be able to avoid daily contact with their harassers by changing their academic programs—though only at considerable cost to themselves. These options are less available to students in secondary and graduate institutions, of course, and largely unavailable to students in elementary schools. As a result, students have found protection from sexual harassers only through the resources provided by their schools, colleges, and universities—through policies that are enforced by affirmative action officers, legal counsels, or investigative panels.

For these reasons only a handful of lawsuits have been brought against colleges and universities under Title IX (Schullman and Watts 1990; Watts 1996). In 1992, for example, a U.S. Circuit Court decision on the harassment of students under Title IX had been handed down. And in that decision, *Alexander v. Yale University*, the circuit court seemed to uphold the district court's opinion that a university could not ordinarily be held accountable when an instructor or some other employee harassed a student (as an employer is generally liable for the actions of a supervisor and often for a coworker).

In 1992, however, the Supreme Court extended Title IX's protections for students well beyond any previous court ruling. In a unanimous ruling, the court upheld the suit of a high school student, Christine Franklin, against her high school. She claimed that the school had failed to protect her against persistent sexual harassment by a male teacher, harassment that included rape. A federal trial court had dismissed the case, stating that she could not sue for damages under Title IX. The Supreme Court ruled that she could sue for damages and did not limit the amount she could be awarded. Not only did the Supreme Court hold a school system liable for the sexual harassment of its employees; it permitted damage awards that could far exceed those permitted under Title VII.

ADDITIONAL LEGAL ISSUES

"The Objective Standard"

In order for the courts to make a determination of when an environment reaches the discriminatory level, the courts use an objective test with regard to the effect of the conduct or behavior. The decision as to whether terms or conditions of employment have been changed must be made using an objective perspective: that of an average or reasonable and not a hypersensitive individual. In other words, would a reasonable person be affected? This decision is often dependent on whose perspective is used: a reasonable woman or a reasonable man.

Psychological research suggests that men and women experience, view, react to, and deal with behaviors differently. Thus, the same conduct, if viewed from the perspective of a reasonable woman may have quite a different effect than if judged from the perspective of a reasonable man.

The Supreme Court has stated that it is important that an objective view of the environment be used to judge whether it is discriminatory; it has not made clear whether this objective view is male- or female-oriented or some combination of the two. Thus, lower courts are free to make this determination on their own.

In the *Ellison* case, the court specifically stated that it was viewing the conduct directed at Ms. Ellison through the eyes of a "reasonable woman." The court also stated that this was the only correct way to decide these cases and directed the courts in the ninth circuit to use the "reasonable woman" standard in sexual harassment lawsuits involving a female plaintiff and a claim of "hostile environment." Other courts have also taken this approach, e.g., *Lipsett v. University of Puerto Rico, Andrews v. City of Philadelphia, Burns v. McGregor Elec. Indus., Inc.,* and *Robinson v. Jacksonville Shipyards.*

We refer you to the resources listed in appendix 1 and 2 for additional information about sexual harassment from a legal perspective.

REFERENCES

Bennett-Alexander, D. D. 1987. The Supreme Court Finally Speaks on the Issue of Sexual Harassment—What Did It Say? *Women's Rights Law Reporter* 10: 65–78.

Levy, A., and M. A. Paludi. 1997. *Workplace Sexual Harassment.* Englewood Cliffs, NJ: Prentice Hall.

Lindgren, J. R., and N. Taub. 1988. *The Law of Sex Discrimination.* St. Paul, MN: West Publishing.

Paludi, M. A., ed. 1996. *Sexual Harassment on College Campuses: Abusing the Ivory Power.* Albany: State University of New York Press.

Petrocelli, W., and B. Repa. 1995. *Sexual Harassment on the Job: What It Is and How to Stop It.* Berkeley, CA: Nolo Press.

Shullman, S., and B. Watts. 1990. Legal Issues. In *Ivory Power: Sexual Harassment on Campuses.* Edited by M. A. Paludi. Albany: State University of New York Press.

Watts, B. 1996. Legal Issues. In *Sexual Harassment on College Campuses: Abusing the Ivory Power.* Edited by M. A. Paludi. Albany: State University of New York Press.

Index

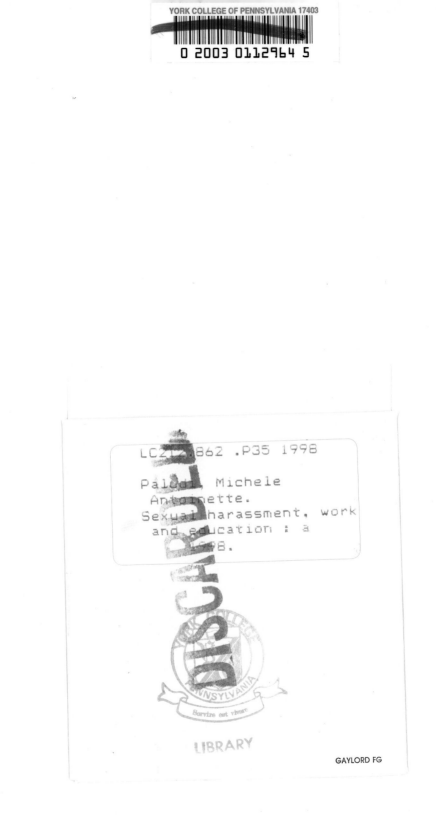